Green Wars The Veggie Vendetta

Green Wars The Veggie Vendetta

Olivia K

UNIEK ENTERPRISES

CONTENTS

Table of Content

Introduction

1. Meet the Protagonist
2. Introduce the main character, an unlikely hero in a world dominated by a powerful vegetable conglomerate.
3. Establish the setting—a dystopian future where vegetables have taken over as the primary source of power and influence.

Chapter 1: The Rise of Veggie Corp

1.1 Explore the history of Veggie Corp

1.2 How did vegetables become the dominant force in society?

1.3 Highlight the charismatic leader of Veggie Corp and their ambitious plans for a veggie-dominated world

.

Chapter 2: The Rebellion Begins

2.1 The Protagonist's Awakening

2.2 The main character discovers the dark secrets behind Veggie Corp.

2.3 Motivated by a personal vendetta, the protagonist decides to take a stand against the vegetable overlords.

Chapter 3: Gathering Allies

3.1 Assembling a Diverse Team

3.2 The protagonist recruits a group of unlikely allies, each with unique skills and backgrounds.

3.3 Develop the relationships and dynamics within the team.

Chapter 4: The Quest for Forbidden Fruit

4.1 Searching for a Legendary Artifact

4.2 The team embarks on a quest to find the forbidden fruit—a mysterious item rumored to have the power to counter Veggie Corp's influence.

4.3 Along the way, they face various challenges and encounters with vegetable enforcers.

Chapter 5: Undercover Operations

5.1 Infiltrating Veggie Corp

5.2 The team devises a plan to infiltrate Veggie Corp's headquarters.

5.3 Uncover Veggie Corp's nefarious plans and the true extent of their control.

Chapter 6: The Battle for Veggie Supremacy

6.1 Showdown at Veggie Corp HQ

6.2 The team confronts Veggie Corp in an epic showdown.

6.3 Highlight the intense battles, clever strategies, and unexpected twists.

Chapter 7: The Aftermath

7.1 Consequences and Fallout

7.2 Explore the aftermath of the battle and the impact on the world.

7.3 Address the changes in society and the characters' personal growth.

Chapter 8: Epilogue

8.1 Seeds of Change

8.2 Conclude the story with a glimpse into the new world order.

8.3 Leave room for the possibility of future adventures or developments in the world of vegetables and rebellion.

Chapter 9: Rebuilding Society

9.1 Explore how the defeat of Veggie Corp leads to a restructuring of society.

1. Highlight the challenges and opportunities that arise as people transition away from vegetable dominance.

9.2 The Legacy of the Veggie Vendetta

1. Examine how the events of the Veggie Vendetta have left a lasting impact on the world.
2. Discuss the lessons learned and the lingering effects on the characters and society.

9.3 A Glimpse into the Future

1. Provide a sneak peek into what lies ahead for the characters and the world they've reshaped.
2. Tease potential new challenges or adventures, keeping the door open for future stories in the Green Wars universe.

Chapter 1

The Rise of Veggie Corp

The Ascent of Veggie Corp: A Green Realm's Climb to Predominance

In the tragic embroidery of "Green Conflicts: The Veggie Grudge," the ascent of Veggie Corp remains as an essential section in the story, unfurling against the setting of an existence where vegetables have turned into the predominant power deeply shaping society's predetermination. In this investigation, we dig into the beginnings, desires, and many-sided maneuvers that pushed Veggie Corp to the pinnacle of force, cementing its status as a considerable element directing the course of mankind's destiny.

The beginning of Veggie Corp follows back to the turbulent period set apart by ecological emergencies, asset exhaustion, and the dire requirement for elective wellsprings of energy. As the conventional mainstays of force disintegrated under the heaviness of natural disregard, a visionary business person, Dr. Cornelius Greenstem, rose up out of the shadows with a progressive thought - saddling the undiscovered possibility of vegetables to support the world as well as to employ uncommon impact.

Dr. Greenstem, a splendid researcher with a foundation in natural chemistry, perceived the inborn energy put away inside vegetables as a generally undiscovered asset. His bold vision tried to change the modest vegetable from a dietary staple into the key part of another time of supportable power. Veggie Corp was considered not just as a partnership but rather as a campaign, a mission to reshape the world's energy scene and, thusly, rethink the overall influence on a worldwide scale.

The early long stretches of Veggie Corp were described by eager examination, trial and error, and the faithful commitment of Dr. Greenstem and his group of spearheading researchers. The partnership's base camp, a rambling complex settled in the midst of fastidiously kept up with fields of exploratory yields, turned into the focal point of a green unrest. Here, the limits among lab and farmland obscured, as researchers worked to open the insider facts of Vege-nergy - a progressive innovation that would saddle the dormant power inside vegetables.

The advancement came as a historic revelation: the extraction of bioelectric energy from vegetables through an interaction known as "chloro-electrogenesis." This leading edge permitted Veggie Corp to foster an inexhaustible and reasonable energy source that could be tackled for a monstrous scope. The ramifications were faltering, as Vege-nergy arose as the cure to a world wavering near the very edge of ecological breakdown.

Veggie Corp's rising to predominance was not simply an innovative victory but rather a determined introduction to the passageways of force. Dr. Greenstem's essential coalitions with compelling political figures, business analysts, and news tycoons prepared for Veggie Corp's consistent mix into the worldwide power structure. The partnership's message of natural salvation and energy supportability resounded with a world frantic for arrangements, situating Veggie Corp as a considerate hero according to the general population.

The rebranding of vegetables as more than simple food however as the way to worldwide advancement became Veggie Corp's mantra. Promotion crusades, supported research studies, and decisively positioned powerhouses overwhelmed the open arena, molding a story that situated Veggie Corp as the vanguard of a green perfect world. The organization's logo, an adapted vegetable enclosed by leaves, turned into a seal of trust, a symbol that enhanced everything from energy-effective machines to government-endorsed writing.

Veggie Corp's financial impact was solidified through a snare of auxiliaries, consolidations, and key acquisitions that spread over the horticultural, innovation, and drug areas. The partnership's command over the creation, circulation, and exploration of vegetables turned out to be outright, further setting its status as an unassailable power. In the financial domain, Veggie Corp was not simply a player but rather a manikin ace, calling the shots of worldwide business sectors with determined artfulness.

As Veggie Corp's impact developed, so did its effect on cultural designs. The company's obligation to supportability turned into the outline for metropolitan preparation, with urban areas updated to integrate vertical ranches, green rooftops, and tank-farming frameworks. The compositional scene turned into a demonstration of Veggie Corp's vision of fitting metropolitan improvement with farming supportability. The outcome was a juxtaposition of transcending high rises decorated with hanging gardens, making a cityscape that reflected the verdant concordance Veggie Corp tried to engender.

The company's venture reached out into instruction, where Veggie Corp-supported educational plans turned into the standard. The more youthful age was taught on the ideals of ecological stewardship, manageability, and the vital job of vegetables in getting a prosperous future. Veggie Corp's impact over instructive foundations, from primary schools to colleges, guaranteed the teaching of ages into a perspective that lined up with the company's plan.

Veggie Corp's mechanical developments reached out past Vegenergy, saturating each part of day to day existence. The coming of bio-based materials got from vegetables reformed ventures like design, development, and transportation. The organization's innovative work arm turned into a favorable place for momentous innovations, every development building up Veggie Corp's situation as a kind gatekeeper of mankind's future.

Be that as it may, the story uncovers the more obscure underside of Veggie Corp's ascent to strength. The company's facade of generosity covers a determined quest for benefit, an unquenchable craving for control, and a dismissal for the drawn out natural results of its monoculture-driven rehearses. The rambling fields of hereditarily altered vegetables, enhanced for greatest yield and productivity, definite a biological cost for the dirt, water assets, and biodiversity.

As Veggie Corp combined its power, disagree turned into a badly arranged obstruction to its terrific plan. The organization, in agreement with consistent state run administrations, authorized rigid measures to stifle resistance and disagreeing voices. Activists who addressed Veggie Corp's ecological effect or supported for elective energy sources regarded themselves as minimized, hushed, or marked as foes of progress.

The story presents a cast of characters who become reluctant pawns in Veggie Corp's fabulous account. Ranchers, when the stewards of different rural scenes, end up forced into embracing Veggie Corp's hereditarily altered crops, their customary practices eclipsed by the organization's monoculture juggernaut. The dislodging of nearby cultivating networks turns into a powerful image of the cost paid for Veggie Corp's command.

The ascent of Veggie Corp, while a demonstration of human creativity, turns into a wake up call about the risks of uncontrolled corporate power. The company's extremely tight grip on worldwide assets, its control of public discernment, and the concealment of dispute bring up issues about the moral ramifications of depending on a solitary element for the food of society. The story provokes perusers to ponder the sensitive harmony between mechanical progression, corporate impact, and ecological supportability.

As Veggie Corp's predominance turns out to be outright, the story movements to the rise of the Veggie Feud — not entirely set in stone to challenge the organization's authority. The contention between Veggie Corp and the Veggie Grudge turns into the support whereupon the story turns, pushing the story into an arresting investigation of force, obstruction, and the getting through battle for a maintainable future.

1.1 Explore the history of Veggie Corp

Developing Territory: Uncovering the Underlying foundations of Veggie Corp's Authority

In the tragic scene of "Green Conflicts: The Veggie Grudge," the historical backdrop of Veggie Corp unfurls as an adventure unpredictably woven into the texture of cultural change. This investigation digs into the starting points, development, and the unpredictable embroidery of occasions that finished in the ascent of Veggie Corp — a corporate monster that would employ unrivaled impact, shape worldwide stories, and become the orchestrator of a green upset that would generally change the direction of human civilization.

The beginning of Veggie Corp can be followed back to the mid 21st hundred years, a period set apart by expanding ecological mindfulness, heightening worries about environmental change, and a developing acknowledgment of the unreasonableness of existing horticultural and energy rehearses. In this time, Dr. Cornelius Greenstem, a visionary organic chemist intensely for economical living, left on an extraordinary excursion that would ultimately prompt the foundation of Veggie Corp.

Dr. Greenstem's initial life was set apart by a well established love for nature and a voracious interest in the unpredictable operations of the climate. Brought up in an agrarian local area that was wrestling with the outcomes of modern agribusiness, he saw firsthand the corruption of soil, the deficiency of biodiversity, and the ecological cost claimed by regular cultivating rehearses. These encounters energized Dr. Greenstem's assurance to find inventive arrangements that could orchestrate human life with the regular world.

Driven by his obligation to supportability, Dr. Greenstem committed a very long time to investigating elective energy sources and more eco-accommodating farming practices. His leading edge second came when he disentangled the undiscovered capacity inside vegetables — a wellspring of bioelectric energy that could reform the worldwide energy scene. With this revelation, Dr. Greenstem established the groundwork for Veggie Corp, imagining it not only as a corporate element but rather as an impetus for cultural and natural change.

The early long periods of Veggie Corp were set apart by an intense quest for logical development and trial and error. Dr. Greenstem gathered a group of similar researchers, engineers, and farming specialists who shared his vision of bridling the inert power inside vegetables. Their undertakings prompted the improvement of Vege-nergy, a notable innovation that could concentrate and change over the bioelectric energy put away in vegetables into a sustainable and supportable power source.

Veggie Corp's innovative advancement accumulated consideration, not just for its capability to change the energy area yet additionally for its arrangement with the prospering natural development. Dr. Greenstem, a magnetic nonentity, turned into the substance of Veggie Corp's central goal, articulating a dream of a future where mankind flourished as one with nature. The enterprise's initial promoting efforts underlined environmental obligation, supportability, and the commitment of a greener, more prosperous world.

As Veggie Corp picked up speed, its desires extended past the domain of energy. Perceiving the interconnectedness of farming, innovation, and cultural designs, the company enhanced its endeavors. Veggie Corp's agrarian exploration divisions dove into hereditary adjustment, upgrading vegetable harvests for greatest yield, strength, and versatility to assorted environments. The enterprise's introduction to farming strength laid the foundation for its later impact over worldwide food creation.

In the socio-political scene, Veggie Corp decisively developed partnerships with compelling figures, lawmakers, and key chiefs. Dr. Greenstem's vision resounded with those looking for answers for the squeezing difficulties of ecological debasement and asset exhaustion. The partnership's reconciliation into political circles permitted it to shape strategies great for its targets, making a cooperative relationship that would strengthen Veggie Corp's situation as an impressive player in worldwide issues.

Veggie Corp's rising to unmistakable quality resembled a change in open cognizance. The company's informing, scattered through different media channels, depicted vegetables as a dietary need as well as the foundation of a manageable and agreeable future. Veggie Corp became inseparable from progress, advancement, and natural obligation, steadily penetrating the aggregate mind of social orders all over the planet.

In the financial field, Veggie Corp utilized its impact to lay out an imposing business model over the creation, dissemination, and examination of vegetables. The organization's auxiliaries, acquisitions, and vital associations made an interconnected web that spread over landmasses. Veggie Corp's command over rural stockpile chains allowed it phenomenal power, empowering the company to control market elements and direct the particulars of worldwide exchange.

The organization's introduction to innovation stretched out past Vege-nergy. Veggie Corp's innovative work arms investigated bioplastics, biofuels, and a horde of uses for vegetable-inferred materials. This mechanical expansion further hardened Veggie Corp's impact, as the organization's developments pervaded enterprises going from style to development, laying out it as a dauntless power in molding the eventual fate of different areas.

The defining moment in Veggie Corp's set of experiences accompanied the presentation of Vege-Web, a refined organization of interconnected frameworks that worked with the consistent trade of data, assets, and innovations. Vege-Web rose above public lines, making a worldwide framework that permitted Veggie Corp to apply impact and control on a phenomenal scale. The enterprise's mechanical ability and broad organization raised it to the situation with a worldwide hegemon, with Vege-Web filling in as the operational hub of Veggie Corp's domain.

Nonetheless, as Veggie Corp's impact extended, so did the ecological results of its practices. The organization's monoculture-driven farming model, dependent on hereditarily changed crops improved for yield, prompted the consumption of soil ripeness, loss of biodiversity, and natural corruption for an enormous scope. The very rehearses that Veggie Corp advocated as answers for natural difficulties became wellsprings of conflict as ecological activists, researchers, and minimized networks raised worries about the secret expenses of Veggie Corp's predominance.

As difference stewed underneath the surface, Veggie Corp answered with a determined technique of co-optation and concealment. The enterprise subsidized research drives that lined up with its account, defamed contradicting perspectives, and decisively moved to quiet disagreeing voices. The story presents characters who, regardless of their reservations, end up entrapped in Veggie Corp's snare of impact, featuring the tricky idea of the organization's control.

The peak of Veggie Corp's set of experiences corresponds with the development of the Veggie Feud — an underground development that challenges the enterprise's authority. The story's center movements to the contention between Veggie Corp and the Veggie Quarrel, investigating the crash of philosophies, the intricacies of force elements, and the persevering through battle for ecological equity in a world eclipsed by corporate predominance.

1.2 How did vegetables become the dominant force in society?

From Ranch to Authority: The Impossible Command of Vegetables in Cultural Strength

In the speculative universe of "Green Conflicts: The Veggie Feud," the progress of vegetables from dietary staples to the transcendent power forming cultural fate is a many-sided story of natural emergency, mechanical advancement, and corporate moving. This investigation digs into the variables and occasions that coordinated this change in outlook, disentangling the development of vegetables from humble harvests to the key part of a tragic reality where they rule.

The beginning of vegetables as a prevailing power in the public eye can be followed back to a basic point in the mid 21st hundred years. The world was wrestling with the outcomes of unrestrained industrialization, wild deforestation, and the approaching apparition of environmental change. Conventional wellsprings of energy were demonstrating impractical, and a worldwide agreement arose on the earnest need to progress towards sustainable and eco-accommodating other options.

It was in this cauldron of ecological criticalness that the visionary natural chemist, Dr. Cornelius Greenstem, set out on a groundbreaking mission. Driven by an energy for maintainable residing and a well established love for nature, he imagined a future where humankind could coincide agreeably with the climate. Perceiving the undiscovered possibility inside vegetables, Dr. Greenstem set off on a mission to reclassify the job of these modest yields in the excellent embroidery of human civilization.

The primary impetus in the ascendency of vegetables was the progressive forward leap in bridling bioelectric energy from these plants. Dr. Greenstem's examination, upheld by a group of spearheading researchers, prompted the improvement of Vege-nergy — a notable innovation that could concentrate, convert, and use the intrinsic energy put away inside vegetables. This groundbreaking revelation laid the basis for another time where vegetables wouldn't just be a wellspring of food however a foundation of worldwide power.

Vege-nergy ended up being a unique advantage, offering an inexhaustible and manageable energy source that could moderate the ecological effect of customary energy creation. As conventional energy sources confronted expanding investigation for their commitment to environmental change, Vege-nergy arose as an encouraging sign — a spotless, green arrangement that could drive social orders without compromising the planet's prosperity.

The second consider the ascent of vegetables as a prevailing power was the determined incorporation of this innovation into the worldwide power structure. Dr. Greenstem, with his magnetic vision and vital keenness, manufactured collusions with powerful political figures, financial experts, and news head honchos. This alliance building permitted the incipient Veggie Corp to consistently incorporate into the halls of force, molding approaches and public talk to line up with its vision.

The public's receptivity to Veggie Corp's message was the third vital component in the power of vegetables. The company's showcasing efforts, supported by significant monetary ventures, changed the impression of vegetables in the public awareness. Vegetables stopped being unremarkable dietary decisions and became images of progress, ecological obligation, and an idealistic vision for an amicable conjunction among humankind and nature.

The fourth figure this extraordinary excursion was Veggie Corp's broadening past energy creation. Perceiving the interconnectedness of agribusiness, innovation, and cultural designs, the organization extended its scope. Veggie Corp's rural examination divisions dove into hereditary change, advancing vegetables for greatest yield, versatility, and flexibility. This essential move established the groundwork for the enterprise's impact over worldwide food creation, getting its job as the sole judge of vegetable-related advances.

In the socio-political domain, Veggie Corp's impact stretched out past its mechanical ability. The company utilized its financial could to lay out a syndication over the creation, dispersion, and examination of vegetables. Auxiliaries, acquisitions, and vital organizations made a many-sided web that crossed the globe, permitting Veggie Corp to control market elements and direct the details of worldwide exchange. The enterprise's command over horticultural stock chains allowed it uncommon power, empowering it to impact political choices and shape the direction of countries.

The fifth impetus in vegetables' ascent to predominance was the social rebranding organized by Veggie Corp. The company's impact saturated each aspect of day to day existence, from culinary practices to form decisions. Eateries embraced vegetable-based foods, style enterprises integrated plant-based materials, and cultural standards moved to commend the eco-accommodating way of life upheld by Veggie Corp. Vegetables turned out to be more than food; they became images of status, progress, and adherence to the partnership's vision for a green perfect world.

The 6th component was Veggie Corp's mechanical developments stretching out past energy creation. The enterprise's innovative work arms investigated applications for vegetable-determined materials in different ventures.

From bioplastics to biofuels, Veggie Corp's advancements pervaded areas like design, development, and transportation. The enterprise's mechanical expansion invigorated its impact, laying out it as an unyielding power forming the eventual fate of numerous ventures.

The defining moment in the story happened with the presentation of Vege-Web — a complex organization of interconnected frameworks that worked with the consistent trade of data, assets, and advances. Vege-Web rose above public lines, making a worldwide foundation that permitted Veggie Corp to apply impact and control on a phenomenal scale. The organization's mechanical ability and sweeping organization raised it to the situation with a worldwide hegemon, with Vege-Web filling in as the operational hub of Veggie Corp's domain.

Be that as it may, the story presents an intricate inclination of dispute and potentially negative side-effects. As Veggie Corp's impact extended, so did the natural repercussions of its practices. The company's monoculture-driven rural model, dependent on hereditarily changed crops improved for yield, prompted the consumption of soil fruitfulness, loss of biodiversity, and natural corruption for a gigantic scope. The very rehearses that Veggie Corp advocated as answers for biological difficulties became wellsprings of dispute as natural activists, researchers, and minimized networks raised worries about the secret expenses of Veggie Corp's predominance.

Disagree, a seventh variable, arose as a developing propensity that undermined Veggie Corp's painstakingly built story. Activists scrutinized the organization's natural effect, researchers uncovered the biological cost of monoculture cultivating, and underestimated networks endured the worst part of dislodging and environmental corruption. The account presents characters trapped in the crossfire, torn between the charm of Veggie Corp's vision and the unforgiving real factors of its potentially negative side-effects.

As difference stewed underneath the surface, Veggie Corp answered with a determined system of co-optation and concealment. The company supported research drives that lined up with its story, defamed restricting perspectives, and decisively moved to quiet disagreeing voices. The account presents characters who, regardless of their reservations, end up entrapped in Veggie Corp's trap of impact, featuring the slippery idea of the enterprise's control.

The finish of these interconnected variables carries the account to its apex — the development of the Veggie Quarrel. The development turns into an image of opposition, testing the story built by Veggie Corp and upholding for a re-visitation of feasible farming practices. The contention between Veggie Corp and the Veggie Feud turns into the support whereupon the account turns, pushing the story into an arresting investigation of force, obstruction, and the getting through battle for a feasible future.

1.3 Highlight the charismatic leader of Veggie Corp and their ambitious plans for a veggie-dominated world.

In the unpredictable embroidered artwork of "Green Conflicts: The Veggie Quarrel," the alluring head of Veggie Corp, Dr. Cornelius Greenstem, arises as a focal figure whose vision and attraction push the company to remarkable levels. This investigation dives into the cryptic persona of Dr. Greenstem, his visionary designs for a veggie-overwhelmed world, and the charming charm that spellbinds the majority, reshaping cultural discernments and power elements.

Dr. Cornelius Greenstem, the forebear of Veggie Corp, epitomizes a remarkable mix of logical keenness, natural cognizance, and magnetic initiative. From the beginning of his vision, Dr. Greenstem looked for to alter the energy scene as well as to reclassify mankind's relationship with nature. His process starts with a well established love for the climate, developed in his early stages inside an agrarian local area wrestling with the outcomes of modern farming.

The account winds around the narrative of Dr. Greenstem's initial life, his scholastic interests in natural chemistry, and the urgent minutes that energized his assurance to track down feasible arrangements. The personality of Dr. Greenstem is formed by a significant feeling of obligation — a conviction that humankind should blend with the regular world as opposed to take advantage of it. This ethical compass turns into the main thrust behind his tenacious quest for elective energy sources, at last prompting the weighty revelation of Vege-nergy.

Dr. Greenstem's charming authority becomes clear in his capacity to express a convincing vision that reverberates with a world on the cliff of ecological emergency. His addresses, loaded down with energy and criticalness, catch the creative mind of legislators, persuasive figures, and the overall population the same. The appealling atmosphere encompassing Dr. Greenstem turns into a gravitational power, bringing people from different foundations into the overlap of Veggie Corp's central goal.

Fundamental to Dr. Greenstem's aggressive plans is the rethinking of vegetables not simply as dietary necessities but rather as the key part of an idealistic vision for cultural change. The magnetic pioneer imagines an existence where vegetables are the way to feasible residing, clean energy, and biological congruity. His desire rises above the traditional limits of corporate achievement, developing into a mission to reshape the actual texture of human progress.

The account digs into Dr. Greenstem's essential partnerships with persuasive figures in legislative issues, financial aspects, and media. His capacity to explore the hallways of force, combined with a certified faith in the groundbreaking capability of Vege-nergy, permits Veggie Corp to flawlessly coordinate into the worldwide power structure.

Dr. Greenstem's appeal turns into an impetus for alliance building, transforming Veggie Corp into a partnership as well as an imposing power molding the direction of countries.

As Veggie Corp picks up speed, Dr. Greenstem's vision stretches out past Vege-nergy, including a diverse way to deal with cultural predominance. The alluring pioneer perceives the interconnectedness of agribusiness, innovation, and social insights. His arrangements include tackling vegetable-inferred energy as well as upgrading vegetable harvests through hereditary alteration, invading ventures through imaginative innovations, and rebranding vegetables as images of progress and supportability.

The magnetic charm of Dr. Greenstem assumes a significant part in Veggie Corp's social rebranding. Through designated showcasing efforts, the magnetic pioneer changes vegetables into seals of a green perfect world. Eateries embrace vegetable-based foods, design businesses take on plant-based materials, and cultural standards shift to commend the eco-accommodating way of life upheld by Dr. Greenstem. The alluring pioneer's capacity to transform vegetables into superficial points of interest further sets Veggie Corp's impact, forming customer ways of behaving and cultural qualities.

Veggie Corp's charming chief turns into the essence of a worldwide development, a nonentity inseparable from progress, development, and natural obligation. Dr. Greenstem's media presence, from meetings to public locations, cultivates a feeling of trust and reverence. The charming pioneer's validness, combined with a certifiable obligation to a practical future, makes a story that enthralls hearts and brains across the globe.

As Veggie Corp's alluring chief, Dr. Greenstem presents Vege-Web — a complex organization that concretes the company's strength on a worldwide scale. The story investigates the essential brightness behind this innovative wonder, stressing Dr. Greenstem's foreknowledge in making a framework that works with consistent data trade, asset conveyance, and mechanical headways. Vege-Web turns into the operational hub of Veggie Corp's domain, solidifying the magnetic pioneer's vision into an unmistakable organization of impact.

However, underneath the charming facade lies a nuanced depiction of Dr. Greenstem's personality. The story explores the unseen struggles and moral quandaries looked by the alluring pioneer as Veggie Corp's impact grows. The accidental ecological outcomes of monoculture cultivating, disagreeing voices inside established researchers, and the removal of underestimated networks present moral dilemmas that add layers to Dr. Greenstem's personality.

As dispute stews underneath the surface, Dr. Greenstem's reaction turns into a basic part of the story. The charming pioneer, mindful of the difficulties presented by disagreeing voices, utilizes a determined methodology of co-optation and concealment. Research drives lined up with Veggie Corp's account are supported, restricting perspectives are ruined, and it are decisively underestimated to disagree voices. This more obscure side of the magnetic pioneer's strategies brings up issues about the morals of impact and the results of unrestrained power.

The peak of the story combines on the rise of the Veggie Grudge — a development testing Veggie Corp's authority. The appealling pioneer's vision slams into the opposition of the individuals who question the account built by Dr. Greenstem. The contention turns into a cauldron where philosophies conflict, power elements are tried, and the magnetic pioneer's vision faces its most imposing test.

2

Chapter 2

The Rebellion Begins

Seeds of Dispute: The Beginning of Resistance To Veggie Corp

In the tragic story of "Green Conflicts: The Veggie Grudge," the resistance to Veggie Corp unfurls as a multi-layered adventure, winding around together the strings of difference, natural cognizance, and the dauntless soul of the people who try to challenge the veggie-overwhelmed business as usual. This investigation digs into the beginning of the resistance, the characters who catalyze change, and the heightening clash that shapes the account's direction.

The insubordination to Veggie Corp grows from the seeds of difference planted by people who will not acknowledge the account made by the appealling pioneer, Dr. Cornelius Greenstem. These protesters, from different foundations and inspirations, join to shape the Veggie Feud — a not entirely set in stone to uncover the hazier underside of Veggie Corp's predominance and backer for a re-visitation of supportable farming practices.

The story presents a cast of characters who become impetuses for the insubordination. Among them is Dr. Elena Meadowlark, a splendid ecological researcher baffled by Veggie Corp's concealment of dispute inside mainstream researchers. Dr. Meadowlark turns into a vital figure in disentangling the ecological outcomes of Veggie Corp's monoculture-driven rehearses. Her excursion from a once-regarded researcher inside the Veggie Corp research crease to an informant uncovered the inner gaps inside the enterprise.

Another focal person is Jackson Thornfield, a previous rancher uprooted by Veggie Corp's forceful farming practices. Thornfield's association with the land, his deficiency of work, and the relocation of his local area become the main impetus behind his contribution in the Veggie Grudge. His process represents the human expense of Veggie Corp's uncontrolled predominance, adding an impactful aspect to the defiance.

As the insubordination picks up speed, the story investigates the complexities of Veggie Corp's reaction to disagree. Dr. Greenstem, the charming pioneer, sends a mix of co-optation and concealment to kill resistance. Contradicting voices are minimized, elective perspectives are ruined, and Veggie Corp's impact stretches out into the halls of ability to shape strategies that favor the company. The insubordination turns into a David-and-Goliath battle against a solid substance using unrivaled impact.

The Veggie Feud's beginning is set apart by secret gatherings, encoded correspondence channels, and the cautious coordination of endeavors to uncover Veggie Corp's hazier side. The disobedience uses Vege-Web, the very network that works with Veggie Corp's worldwide predominance, to disperse data uncovering the natural cost, concealment of dispute, and moral omissions inside the organization. The utilization of innovation turns into a useful asset for the dissidents, empowering them to explore the computerized scene and prepare support.

The insubordination's topical center spins around the conflict between beliefs — Veggie Corp's vision of progress, development, and natural obligation versus the Veggie Feud's call for straightforwardness, responsibility, and a re-visitation of supportable farming practices. The account investigates the philosophical underpinnings of each side, bringing up issues about the moral ramifications of unrestrained corporate power and the fragile harmony between mechanical advancement and natural stewardship.

The defiance's rise concurs with a change in open opinion. As data dispersed by the Veggie Quarrel builds up momentum, public view of Veggie Corp starts to crack. The once-unchallenged story of a green ideal world is presently obfuscated by disclosures of natural corruption, removal of networks, and the concealment of difference. The resistance's prosperity lies in uncovering Veggie Corp's offenses as well as in reshaping public discernment and stirring help for an elective vision.

The account unpredictably winds through the existences of conventional residents who, notwithstanding affliction, line up with the Veggie Quarrel. The resistance turns into an aggregate undertaking, rising above individual inspirations and foundations. From metropolitan activists utilizing online entertainment to ranchers opposing the constrained reception of hereditarily changed crops, the disobedience resounds with a different cross-segment of society. The story underlines the widespread allure of the Veggie Feud's message — a call for responsibility, equity, and a reexamination of mankind's relationship with the climate.

The contention raises as Veggie Corp, compromised by the insubordination's developing impact, conveys countermeasures. The company increases its endeavors to stifle contradict, depicting the Veggie Grudge as a periphery development hawking deception. Dr. Greenstem, the alluring pioneer, turns into the public substance of Veggie Corp's safeguard, endeavoring to ruin the disobedience and reassert command over the account. The story capably depicts the power elements at play, as Veggie Corp's impact conflicts with the renegades' assurance to uncover reality.

The insubordination's account circular segment is set apart by snapshots of pressure, key moving, and unanticipated partnerships. The Veggie Feud, when a unique gathering of nonconformists, combines into an imposing power testing Veggie Corp's authority. The revolutionaries utilize a mix of digital activism, common insubordination, and grass-roots developments to intensify their message and prepare support. The story constructs a need to get a move on as the dissidents explore the intricacies of their central goal, summoning compassion for their objective.

The peak of the defiance unfurls in a progression of conflicts — both philosophical and physical — between Veggie Corp and the Veggie Quarrel. The story arrives at a crescendo as the radicals uncover Veggie Corp's dishonest practices through spilled records, informants, and public exhibitions. The resistance turns into an image of flexibility, rousing others to scrutinize the norm and request responsibility from the people who use uncontrolled power.

The account doesn't avoid the outcomes of resistance. As the contention escalates, the Veggie Quarrel faces expanding investigation, counter from Veggie Corp, and inner divisions. The agitators wrestle with the ethical intricacies of their main goal, scrutinizing the lengths to which they will go to destroy the very framework they try to oust. The defiance turns into a trial of standards, versatility, and the getting through soul of the individuals who try to challenge the laid out request.

In the goal of the disobedience, the story investigates the fallout of Veggie Corp's openness and the cultural movements that follow. The once-predominant partnership faces public shock, lawful repercussions, and a reexamination of its practices.

The Veggie Quarrel's prosperity lies in destroying Veggie Corp's authority as well as in catalyzing a more extensive discussion about the moral ramifications of corporate power, the significance of ecological stewardship, and the requirement for straightforwardness in molding the eventual fate of society.

The story finishes up with a reflection on the persevering through tradition of the disobedience. While Veggie Corp might have been destroyed, the story recognizes that the battle for a maintainable future is a continuous excursion. The Veggie Quarrel turns into an image of obstruction, motivating people in the future to address authority, challenge settled in power designs, and backer for an existence where progress is inseparable from moral obligation.

2.1 The Protagonist's Awakening

In the rambling story of "Green Conflicts: The Veggie Feud," the hero's enlivening fills in as a significant second, denoting the change of a normal person into a focal figure in the opposition against Veggie Corp. This investigation dives into the excursion of self-disclosure, the impetuses that push the hero into the core of the resistance, and the advancing elements that shape their job in the unfurling adventure.

The hero, at first an onlooker exploring the veggie-ruled world, encounters a slow arousing that is catalyzed by a progression of occasions. The story cautiously follows the hero's everyday presence — maybe a corporate representative, a disappointed researcher, or a dislodged rancher — before the inducing episode sets off an outpouring of acknowledge. This enlivening isn't simply an individual disclosure however a cultural one, divulging the hazier underside of Veggie Corp's strength and the earnest requirement for obstruction.

The hero's process starts with a troubling acknowledgment — a chewing sense that something is wrong in the probably idealistic world created by Veggie Corp. This underlying mindfulness might be ignited by an opportunity experience with a disagreeing voice, a brief look behind the cleaned exterior of Veggie Corp's promoting efforts, or an individual encounter that challenges the acknowledged story. The story cautiously develops a feeling of disquiet, provoking the hero to scrutinize the state of affairs and leave on an excursion of self-disclosure.

The enlivening picks up speed through experiences with key figures in the defiance. The hero might run into Dr. Elena Meadowlark, the natural researcher whose whistleblowing endeavors uncover the ecological outcomes of Veggie Corp's practices. On the other hand, the hero could interface with Jackson Thornfield, the dislodged rancher whose story exemplifies the human expense of Veggie Corp's strength. These experiences become impetuses for the hero's more profound contribution in the obstruction, offering viewpoints that reverberate with their blossoming feeling of discontent.

The account unpredictably winds around the hero's very own battles with the more extensive cultural issues at play. The difficulties looked by the hero — be it moral problems, unseen fits of turmoil, or the feeling of dread toward backlash from Veggie Corp — reflect the battles of people wrestling with the outcomes of corporate strength. The hero's interior process turns into a mirror mirroring the more extensive cultural arousing, highlighting the interconnectedness of individual and aggregate change.

The hero's acknowledgment stretches out past the ecological results of Veggie Corp's practices. The story digs into the moral elements of the hero's excursion, investigating the pressure between private addition and cultural obligation. The enlivening turns into an ethical retribution, driving the hero to defy awkward insights about their own complicity in a framework that focuses on benefit over morals. This moral aspect adds profundity to the hero's personality, raising them from a simple spectator to a functioning member in the opposition.

As the hero's mindfulness extends, the story presents snapshots of thoughtfulness and self-revelation. The hero wrestles with their own weaknesses, predispositions, and biases, defying the intricacies of exploring a world in motion. This interior excursion, intertwined with outer difficulties presented by Veggie Corp's impact, shapes the hero into a nuanced and engaging focal figure whose development reflects the more extensive cultural arousing.

The account utilizes vital pacing to fabricate strain as the hero's enlivening lines up with the heightening of contention between Veggie Corp and the Veggie Grudge. The hero, at first a reluctant member, turns out to be progressively snared in the obstruction's exercises. The enlivening is certainly not an unexpected disclosure however a continuous development, reflecting the natural course of cultural arousing despite corporate strength. This purposeful pacing uplifts the close to home reverberation of the hero's excursion.

The hero's enlivening is set apart by a progression of disclosures about Veggie Corp's concealment of difference, natural debasement, and the partnership's tricky impact over political and financial designs. The story utilizes a mosaic methodology, winding around together parts of data, experiences with key figures, and individual encounters to develop an exhaustive picture. This mosaic of disclosures pushes the hero into the core of the resistance, changing them from a detached eyewitness to a functioning influencer.

The hero's developing contribution in the obstruction is joined by a feeling of strengthening and organization. The story cautiously depicts the hero's change from a place of weakness to one of versatility and assurance. This change isn't without its difficulties — the hero faces dangers, moral issues, and the approaching phantom of Veggie Corp's response. Be that as it may, the hero's enlivening engages them to go up against these difficulties head-on, exemplifying the soul of opposition.

The story presents tutor figures who guide the hero through their enlivening. These coaches might be prepared activists, disappointed previous representatives of Veggie Corp, or people with a profound comprehension of the ecological and moral ramifications of corporate predominance. The coach figures furnish the hero with information, direction, and an ethical compass, forming their excursion and adding to the more extensive subject of aggregate arousing.

The hero's enlivening concurs with a more extensive cultural shift. The story investigates the expanding influences of the Veggie Feud's exercises, specifying how the scattering of data, public exhibits, and demonstrations of common noncompliance add to a groundswell of obstruction. The enlivening turns into a common encounter, joining people from different foundations under the flag of testing Veggie Corp's authority. The story underlines the infectious idea of enlivening, outlining how one person's acknowledgment can catalyze a cascading type of influence that changes society.

The peak of the hero's enlivening happens in a urgent snapshot of conflict with Veggie Corp. This second fills in as a cauldron, testing the hero's purpose, moral convictions, and eagerness to defy the charming pioneer, Dr. Cornelius Greenstem. The story works to a crescendo, catching the force of the hero's inward and outer battles. The enlivening arrives at its peak as the hero, when a detached eyewitness, faces Veggie Corp's impact head-on, typifying the defiance's ethos.

In the repercussions of the peak, the account investigates the outcomes of the hero's enlivening. The hero's activities add to Veggie Corp's openness, the unwinding of the partnership's strength, and the cultural shift toward an additional economical and moral future. The enlivening turns into an impetus for more extensive foundational change, showing the extraordinary force of individual organization inside the setting of aggregate opposition.

The goal of the hero's enlivening is nuanced, keeping away from shortsighted victories or losses. The story recognizes the intricacies of exploring a world experiencing significant change, featuring the continuous difficulties looked by the hero and the more extensive obstruction development. The enlivening, while extraordinary, is depicted as a continuous excursion — one that requires supported exertion, versatility, and a promise to the rules that energized the hero's underlying acknowledgment.

2.2 The main character discovers the dark secrets behind Veggie Corp.

In the complex embroidery of "Green Conflicts: The Veggie Feud," the fundamental person sets out on an excursion of revelation that unwinds the painstakingly built veneer of Veggie Corp, uncovering dull mysteries concealed underneath the surface. This investigation digs into the hero's quest for truth, the disclosures that break assumptions, and the ethical retribution that goes with the openness of Veggie Corp's surreptitious activities.

The story cautiously lays out the fundamental person's underlying impression of Veggie Corp — an apparently generous company proclaiming a green ideal world. The hero, maybe a representative inside Veggie Corp or an accidental customer of its items, explores a world molded by the company's impact. The pure veneer is carefully created, with Veggie Corp introducing itself as a boss of manageability, development, and ecological obligation.

The excursion of revelation starts with a progression of apparently harmless occasions that plant the seeds of uncertainty in the primary person's brain. Maybe it begins with a heard discussion, an opportunity experience with a contradicting voice, or the uncovering of grouped reports. These underlying looks in the background brief the principal character to scrutinize the acknowledged story and set out on a mission for truth.

The hero's quest for truth is laden with difficulties, as Veggie Corp conveys its impact to stifle difference and control the progression of data. The enterprise, when seen as a paragon of straightforwardness, uncovers its dictator propensities, controlling media stories, undermining informants, and applying strain on the people who set out to challenge its strength. The principal character's process turns into an unsafe odyssey, exploring a scene where truth is a scant product.

The story utilizes a mosaic way to deal with disclosure, winding around together pieces of data, experiences with key figures, and incognito examinations. The principal character uncovers a path of breadcrumbs — pieces of information that indicate the more obscure intrigues underneath Veggie Corp's public picture. This mosaic turns into a story gadget, uplifting tension and welcoming perusers to sort out the riddle close by the hero.

The dull insider facts behind Veggie Corp slowly become exposed, and the primary person wrestles with the ethical ramifications of these disclosures. Natural corruption arises as a focal subject, with Veggie Corp's monoculture-driven horticultural works on ending up a wellspring of environmental pulverization. The fundamental person finds the organization's job in deforestation, soil exhaustion, and the relocation of native networks — an ecological cost taken cover behind the green facade of Veggie Corp's showcasing efforts.

One more layer of haziness is divulged as the primary person digs into Veggie Corp's political maneuvers. The partnership's impact reaches out into administrative bodies, administrative offices, and global associations, permitting it to shape approaches that favor its inclinations. The fundamental person uncovers the treacherous nexus between corporate power and political independent direction, uncovering a snare of debasement and control that compromises the actual underpinnings of a majority rules government.

The story presents characters who become critical conductors of data for the principal character. Informants inside Veggie Corp, baffled previous workers, and activists on the edges of society give key bits of knowledge that puncture through the smoke screen. These characters, frequently gambling with their security to share reality, add to the developing collection of proof that ensnares Veggie Corp in a snare of double dealing.

The disclosure of Veggie Corp's dishonest trials turns into a defining moment in the story. The principal character coincidentally finds labs where hereditary change of vegetables takes a dull turn, with outcomes that reach out past horticultural practices. The company's journey for predominance includes messing with the actual texture of nature, prompting unseen side-effects that present existential dangers to biological systems and, possibly, mankind itself.

As the primary person dives further, they stand up to the moral issues implanted in Veggie Corp's activities. The company's determined quest for benefit to the detriment of ecological maintainability, human prosperity, and moral contemplations turns into a focal subject. The principal character wrestles with the ramifications of being complicit in a framework that focuses on corporate interests over everyone's benefit — an ethical retribution that adds profundity to their personality.

The story capably explores the mental cost for the fundamental person as they go up against the heaviness of obligation. The information on Veggie Corp's dull privileged insights turns into a weight, testing the hero's perspective and constraining them to reconsider their place inside the framework. The inner turmoil becomes discernible, catching the profound subtleties of enlivening to awkward insights and the resulting battle to accommodate individual morals with fundamental complicity.

The principal character's revelations agree with the heightening of contention between Veggie Corp and the Veggie Feud. The hero turns into a significant resource for the obstruction, furnished with the information that can uncover Veggie Corp's wrongdoings and excite popular assessment against the enterprise. The account blends the individual excursion of revelation with the more extensive cultural arousing, stressing the interconnectedness of individual organization and aggregate obstruction.

The story works to a climactic showdown as the fundamental person, furnished with obvious proof, faces Veggie Corp's magnetic chief, Dr. Cornelius Greenstem. The disclosure turns into a critical second, testing the actual groundworks of Veggie Corp's strength and the charming pioneer's cautiously organized picture. The principal character turns into an image of opposition, exemplifying the boldness to face power and uncover reality.

The fallout of the disclosure is set apart by a seismic change in the story. Veggie Corp, when an unyielding power, faces public shock, legitimate repercussions, and interior dispute. The dull mysteries that were concealed underneath layers of promulgation are exposed, destroying the enterprise's painstakingly built story. The fundamental person's job in uncovering Veggie Corp's wrongdoings turns into a demonstration of the groundbreaking force of individual organization notwithstanding corporate authority.

The story finishes up with a reflection on the getting through effect of the primary person's revelations. While Veggie Corp might confront ramifications for its activities, the story recognizes the intricacies of exploring a world on the move. The fundamental person's process turns into an impetus for more extensive foundational change, outlining the groundbreaking capability of truth notwithstanding misdirection.

2.3 Motivated by a personal vendetta, the protagonist decides to take a stand against the vegetable overlords.

In the tragic story of "Green Conflicts: The Veggie Grudge," the hero's development from a latent onlooker to a considerable power in the opposition against Veggie Corp is filled by a profoundly private feud. This investigation digs into the impetuses that drive the hero to stand firm, the profound intricacies that support their inspiration, and the extraordinary excursion that prompts a showdown with the vegetable masters.

The story cautiously lays out the foundations of the hero's very own grudge — a characterizing occasion that fills in as the profound support of their change. Maybe it is the departure of a friend or family member because of Veggie Corp's deceptive practices, the obliteration of the hero's job, or a face to face a conflict with the partnership's harsh strategies. Anything the impetus, it turns into the main thrust that electrifies the hero right into it.

The hero's choice to stand firm against the vegetable masters isn't simply a reaction to outside conditions yet an indication of inward unrest. The account explores the profound scene of the hero's mind, investigating the melancholy, outrage, and feeling of treachery that fuel their feud. This close to home center adds profundity to the person, changing them from a simple resistor to an image of disobedience against foundational persecution.

The story cautiously follows the hero's excursion from the underlying shock of their own misfortune to the steady acknowledgment that Veggie Corp isn't a mediator of progress yet a slippery power that goes after the weaknesses of society. The close to home circular segment turns into a story gadget, permitting perusers to identify with the hero's inspirations and figure out the instinctive idea of their quarrel.

Spurred by the individual grudge, the hero goes through a transformation — a change that rises above the limits of individual distress and turns into an impetus for more extensive opposition. The story handily depicts the hero's development, featuring snapshots of contemplation, self-disclosure, and the fashioning of a freshly discovered resolve. The hero's choice to stand firm isn't hasty yet a determined reaction to the acknowledgment that they hold the way to uncovering Veggie Corp's dim insider facts.

The individual feud turns into an ethical basic for the hero, driving them to face the very powers that broke their reality. The account investigates the hero's inward clash as they wrestle with the moral ramifications of obstruction. Inquiries of equity, vengeance, and everyone's benefit become necessary to the hero's inner exchange, adding layers to their personality and the all-encompassing subject of cultural commotion.

The story presents key partners who share the hero's quarrel and become instrumental in their excursion. These partners might incorporate people who have experienced comparative misfortunes, previous Veggie Corp insiders baffled by the enterprise's practices, or activists with a common vision of destroying the vegetable masters. The unions manufactured in the cauldron of shared grudges add to the strength of the obstruction and build up the possibility that aggregate activity is the counteractant to individual misery.

As the hero digs further into the opposition, the story explores the strategic parts of their choice to stand firm. Vital preparation, incognito activities, and the cautious scattering of data become essential to the hero's endeavors to uncover Veggie Corp's wrongdoings. The individual feud changes into a more extensive mission — an undertaking to free society from the hold of vegetable masters and usher in a time of straightforwardness and equity.

The profound cost of the hero's grudge is compared with snapshots of win and kinship inside the obstruction. The story winds around a sensitive harmony between the heaviness of individual misfortune and the expectation inborn in aggregate activity. The hero's choice to stand firm turns into a signal of strength, motivating others to join the reason and challenge the vegetable masters who have long worked without risk of punishment.

The story utilizes pacing as a device to enhance the pressure in the hero's excursion. The choice to stand firm is certainly not a particular occasion however a progression of raising activities that lead to a climactic showdown with Veggie Corp. The story cautiously constructs expectation, permitting perusers to observe the hero's development and the mounting stakes of their quarrel.

The close to home peak of the story happens when the hero, driven by their own quarrel, stands up to Veggie Corp's charming chief, Dr. Cornelius Greenstem. This critical second turns into a cauldron where the hero's melancholy, outrage, and assurance unite. The story catches the power of the showdown, exhibiting the close to home and moral elements of the hero's choice to stand firm against the vegetable masters.

In the repercussions of the showdown, the story investigates the outcomes of the hero's grudge. Veggie Corp, when an unassailable power, faces public investigation, lawful repercussions, and inside disagree. The hero's grudge turns into an impetus for foundational change, representing the groundbreaking force of individual organization despite settled in power structures.

The goal of the hero's grudge is nuanced, staying away from short-sighted victories or losses. The story recognizes the intricacies of exploring a world reshaped by the hero's activities. The individual feud, while a main thrust, turns into a piece of the more extensive embroidery of opposition, leaving space for reflection on the getting through results of testing the vegetable masters.

3

Chapter 3

Gathering Allies

In the rambling story of "Green Conflicts: The Veggie Quarrel," the hero sets out on a basic period of their excursion — gathering partners to reinforce the opposition against Veggie Corp. This investigation digs into the complexities of alliance constructing, the different characters who line up with the hero's objective, and the essential moves utilized to manufacture an imposing power testing the vegetable masters.

As the hero explores the turbulent scene of obstruction, the requirement for partners becomes obvious. The story cautiously lays out the difficulties inborn in taking on a behemoth like Veggie Corp — debasement, reconnaissance, and an organization of impact that reaches out into political and monetary circles. Gathering partners becomes a strategic need as well as an essential basic to offset the mind-boggling force of the vegetable masters.

The story presents a different cluster of characters who become vital partners in the obstruction. These partners might incorporate baffled previous Veggie Corp representatives conscious of the company's internal functions, activists with a common vision of destroying corporate predominance, and people who have straightforwardly endured the side-effects of Veggie Corp's dishonest practices. Each partner brings a remarkable range of abilities, viewpoint, and inspiration to the expanding alliance, adding profundity to the opposition's aggregate character.

One urgent partner is Dr. Elena Meadowlark, the ecological researcher whose whistleblowing endeavors uncovered Veggie Corp's natural corruption. Dr. Meadowlark's logical skill turns into an important resource, furnishing the opposition with experiences into Veggie Corp's environmental effect and the necessary resources to counter the partnership's greenwashing publicity. The story investigates the subtleties of Dr. Meadowlark's choice to line up with the obstruction, diving into her own inspirations and the ethical basic that pushes her to share her insight.

Another key partner is Jackson Thornfield, the dislodged rancher whose association with the land and firsthand experience of Veggie Corp's forceful rural practices make him an intense image of obstruction. Thornfield's process becomes meaningful of the human expense claimed by the vegetable masters. His coalition with the hero adds an instinctive aspect to the opposition, establishing it in the lived encounters of those straightforwardly impacted by Veggie Corp's mastery.

The hero's way to deal with social event partners is set apart by a fragile equilibrium of influence, trust-constructing, and shared goals. The story investigates the specialty of alliance building, depicting the hero as a magnetic and vital pioneer who figures out the significance of different viewpoints inside the obstruction. The partners are not simple pawns but rather people driven by their own convictions, and the story explores the intricacies of fashioning a firm and versatile alliance.

The account utilizes vital pacing to construct strain as the hero attempts to accumulate partners. Each partner is presented with a cautious thought of their history, inspirations, and the interesting commitments they bring to the obstruction. The get-together of partners turns into a story crescendo, increasing expectation for the showdown with Veggie Corp. The pacing permits perusers to observe the steady combination of different voices into an agreeable ensemble of contradiction.

The unions shaped inside the obstruction are not without challenges. The story handily explores the interior elements of the alliance, including philosophical contrasts, private issues, and the inborn pressures that emerge when people with different foundations join against a shared adversary. The hero expects the job of a middle person, exploring the complexities of alliance legislative issues and encouraging a feeling of aggregate reason.

The get-together of partners reaches out past individual characters to incorporate different areas of society. The story investigates the hero's endeavors to assemble support among ranchers disenthralled with Veggie Corp's horticultural practices, researchers frustrated by the concealment of dispute, and normal residents stirred to the dim insider facts taken cover behind the vegetable masters' green veneer. The obstruction turns into an embroidery woven from the strings of different voices, joined by a common longing to challenge Veggie Corp's authority.

Vital partnerships stretch out into startling quarters as the account discloses the hero's endeavors to gather support from persuasive figures inside political and monetary circles. The hero's capacity to explore the passages of force, persuade compelling partners of the opposition's authenticity, and secure assets for the purpose turns into a demonstration of their initiative abilities. The story dives into the practicality expected to shape collusions in reality as we know it where power is amassed in the possession of the vegetable masters.

The opposition use innovation, using Vege-Web — the very network constrained by Veggie Corp — to spread data, coordinate exercises, and intensify the message of contradiction. The story investigates the hero's essential utilization of innovation as an instrument for preparation, stressing the significance of saddling the very frameworks utilized by the vegetable masters to challenge their predominance. Vege-Web turns into a two sided deal, all the while empowering opposition and filling in as a landmark for control.

The hero's social event of partners agrees with the acceleration of contention between Veggie Corp and the opposition. The vegetable masters, compromised by the developing alliance, send countermeasures to smother contradict. The story catches the power of this contention, depicting the obstruction as a strong power that will not be quieted. The get-together of partners turns into a urgent second, making way for the climactic showdown that will decide the destiny of the obstruction and the fate of society.

The peak of the story merges on the showdown between Veggie Corp and the opposition — a skirmish of belief systems, methodologies, and aggregate will. The hero's painstakingly gathered alliance turns into an amazing powerhouse, testing the vegetable masters on numerous fronts. The story works to a crescendo, catching the high-stakes nature of the contention and the strength of the opposition notwithstanding Veggie Corp's endeavors to subdue contradict.

The fallout of the showdown investigates the outcomes of the hero's fruitful social event of partners. Veggie Corp, when an unassailable power, faces a considerable opposition that uncovered its wrongdoings, cracks its impact, and makes way for foundational change. The account cautiously explores the outcome, recognizing both the triumphs and difficulties that go with the hero's endeavors to challenge the vegetable masters.

3.1 Assembling a Diverse Team

In the convincing story of "Green Conflicts: The Veggie Grudge," the hero leaves on a vital mission: gathering a different group to face the vegetable masters, Veggie Corp.

This investigation digs into the hero's essential way to deal with group development, the assorted cast of characters enrolled for the opposition, and the collaborations that rise up out of their novel foundations, abilities, and inspirations.

The story cautiously lays out the hero's acknowledgment of the requirement for a different group to offset Veggie Corp's impressive impact. The vegetable masters, with their broad venture into different areas of society, request a multi-faceted reaction. The hero's essential insight becomes obvious as they consider the significance of collecting a group that mirrors the intricacy of the difficulties presented by Veggie Corp.

The hero's enrollment endeavors stretch out past ordinary obstruction models, staying away from platitudes and generalizations. The story presents characters from assorted different backgrounds, each picked for their extraordinary abilities, points of view, and inspirations. This approach adds profundity to the story, depicting the obstruction as a mosaic of voices instead of a solid power.

One vital individual from the assorted group is Dr. Mei Ling Chen, a splendid technologist with a profound comprehension of Veggie Corp's command over Vege-Web — the pervasive organization that supports the vegetable masters' predominance. Dr. Chen's skill becomes instrumental in exploring the computerized scene, countering Veggie Corp's digital predominance, and involving innovation as a device for preparation and correspondence inside the opposition.

One more essential expansion to the group is Rafael Gutierrez, a magnetic local area coordinator with establishes in the metropolitan activism scene. Rafael's capacity to associate with minimized networks, prepare grassroots help, and challenge Veggie Corp's impact in metropolitan regions turns into an essential resource. The story investigates Rafael's excursion, his encounters in grassroots developments, and the inspirations that drive him to join the opposition.

The hero decisively enlists people with inside information on Veggie Corp's activities. Previous representatives baffled by the organization's untrustworthy practices become priceless resources, giving bits of knowledge into Veggie Corp's inward operations and weaknesses. The account digs into the subtle conflicts of these characters, their choice to break positions with the vegetable masters, and the dangers they take to impart basic data to the opposition.

The hero's way to deal with gathering a different group is set apart by a cautious thought of ranges of abilities and mastery. The obstruction incorporates researchers, programmers, local area coordinators, previous corporate insiders, and people straightforwardly impacted by

Veggie Corp's practices. This essential variety empowers the protection from mount a multi-layered challenge, focusing on Veggie Corp on mechanical, social, financial, and ecological fronts.

The story explores the difficulties intrinsic in group elements, depicting the hero as a capable go between who encourages union among people with different foundations, belief systems, and inspirations. The group turns out to be more than the amount of its parts, with every part contributing an exceptional viewpoint that improves the obstruction's aggregate personality. The story accentuates the significance of cooperation, common regard, and mutual perspective inside the different group.

The hero's enlistment endeavors stretch out past individual abilities to incorporate social, orientation, and ethnic variety. The story highlights the significance of portrayal inside the opposition, perceiving that a different group offers a scope of viewpoints and approaches of real value. The obstruction turns into a microcosm of the more extensive society, testing Veggie Corp's homogenizing impact and stressing the strength got from variety.

As the different group meets up, the account investigates the most common way of fashioning associations and building trust among its individuals. Each character's origin story, inspirations, and weaknesses are painstakingly woven into the account, permitting perusers to understand their singular processes. The connections inside the group become a story point of convergence, highlighting the close to home bonds that fortify the opposition against Veggie Corp.

The account utilizes key pacing to construct strain as the different group blends, making way for the unavoidable conflict with Veggie Corp. Each colleague's presentation turns into a story crescendo, uplifting expectation for the cooperative endeavors that will characterize the obstruction's showdowns with the vegetable masters. The pacing permits perusers to observe the progressive development of a durable and considerable power.

The different group's connections with Veggie Corp become a landmark of belief systems and procedures. The account explores the nuanced elements of opposition, depicting the vegetable masters' endeavors to invade, co-pick, and destroy the assorted group. The colleagues, drawn from different areas of society, become strong protectors against Veggie Corp's strategies, typifying the soul of opposition and flexibility.

The account investigates the individual stakes for each colleague as they go up against Veggie Corp. Characters face outer dangers as well as subtle conflicts, wrestling with the moral intricacies of obstruction, the anxiety toward backlash, and the cost that going up against the vegetable masters takes on their own lives. The variety inside the group reaches out to the nuanced investigation of individual encounters inside the opposition.

The hero's essential way to deal with group arrangement is compared with Veggie Corp's endeavors to keep up with its authority.

The vegetable masters, undermined by the different group's aggregate strength, heighten their endeavors to stifle disagree, control data, and kill the opposition. The story catches the high-stakes nature of the contention, stressing the flexibility and versatility of the different group notwithstanding Veggie Corp's considerable countermeasures.

The peak of the story unites on the showdown between the different group and Veggie Corp — a fight that rises above actual clash and envelops philosophical fighting, mechanical duels, and social preparation. The different group turns into an image of aggregate opposition, testing the vegetable masters on numerous fronts. The story works to a crescendo, catching the force of the conflict and the extraordinary force of a unified, various front against settled in corporate strength.

The fallout of the showdown investigates the outcomes of the assorted group's progress in testing Veggie Corp. The vegetable masters, once apparently strong, face public investigation, lawful repercussions, and inner contradiction. The account cautiously explores the repercussions, recognizing both the victories and difficulties that go with the assorted group's endeavors to destroy the vegetable masters' impact.

3.2 The protagonist recruits a group of unlikely allies, each with unique skills and backgrounds.

In the unfurling story of "Green Conflicts: The Veggie Grudge," the hero embraces a significant mission — enlisting a gathering of improbable partners, each having remarkable abilities and foundations that will add to the opposition against Veggie Corp. This investigation digs into the hero's essential way to deal with collecting this eccentric group, the different characters they select, and the cooperative elements that rise out of the far-fetched association of people with unique qualities and encounters.

The story fastidiously makes way for the hero's enlistment mission by stressing the requirement for a group with different gifts to really challenge Veggie Corp. Perceiving that the vegetable masters employ impact across different areas of society, the hero comprehends the need of gathering a gathering of partners whose singular abilities by and large structure an imposing power against Veggie Corp's strength.

The enlistment cycle starts with an insightful thought of each partner's one of a kind abilities, mastery, and expected commitments to the opposition. The hero's essential methodology is set apart by a comprehension that the obstruction requires a complex reaction to Veggie Corp's diverse impact. This insightful curation of the group's creation turns into a focal story subject, highlighting the hero's capacity to recognize the qualities required for an effective opposition.

One of the impossible partners enlisted by the hero is Max "Shadow" Ramirez, a talented programmer with a propensity for remaining off the framework. Max's mastery in exploring the computerized domain turns into a pivotal resource in countering Veggie Corp's digital strength. The account digs into Max's experience, investigating the inspirations that lead him to join the obstruction and the ethical basic that powers his obligation to testing Veggie Corp's command over data.

Another unpredictable partner is Sylvia "Blast" Rodriguez, a previous insightful columnist known for her brave quest for reality. Sylvia's insightful ability and skill for uncovering corporate bad behavior make her a characteristic fit for the opposition. The story investigates Sylvia's excursion, diving into the occasions that drove her to leave conventional news-casting for a more straightforward showdown with Veggie Corp.

The hero decisively enrolls characters from different backgrounds, each carrying a novel viewpoint to the opposition. Whether it's a frustrated previous worker conscious of Veggie Corp's internal operations, an uprooted rancher with firsthand experience of the company's horticultural practices, or an educated tree hugger energetic about uncovering the environmental outcomes of Veggie Corp's activities, each partner adds to the group's variety and flexibility.

The story handily explores the heroes' connections with these impossible partners, featuring the difficulties innate in persuading people with assorted foundations and inspirations to join the opposition. The enrollment interaction turns into a fragile dance of influence, sympathy, and common perspective. The story highlights the hero's capacity to motivate trust and convey the direness of the obstruction's central goal, at last persuading these unique people to join against Veggie Corp.

The characters' inspirations for joining the opposition fluctuate, adding profundity to the account. Some are driven by private grudges against Veggie Corp, having straightforwardly encountered the enterprise's severe practices. Others are inspired by a feeling of moral obligation, perceiving the moral basic of testing corporate strength. The story investigates the profound intricacies of each character's choice to join the opposition, catching the assorted inspirations that fuel their responsibility.

The improbable partners become something beyond confidants; they structure an affectionate group with shared targets and a presence of mind of direction. The story dives into the developing elements inside the gathering, depicting the development of fellowship, common regard, and a mutual perspective of the stakes engaged with testing

Veggie Corp. The group turns into a microcosm of the more extensive obstruction, mirroring the variety and interconnectedness innate in the battle against the vegetable masters.

As the hero's enlistment mission advances, the account investigates the essential advantages of each partner's extraordinary abilities. Whether it's Maximum's capacity to penetrate Veggie Corp's computerized guards, Sylvia's talent for analytical news-casting, or the uprooted rancher's personal information on rural practices, each partner's skill becomes instrumental in the opposition's showdowns with Veggie Corp. The story cautiously meshes these singular commitments into the bigger embroidery of the obstruction's methodology.

The assorted foundations of the far-fetched partners add to the flexibility and versatility of the opposition. The account depicts the group's capacity to explore different territories — metropolitan, rustic, advanced, and biological — mirroring the multi-layered nature of Veggie Corp's impact. The group turns into a living demonstration of the hero's foreknowledge in gathering a gathering fit for testing the vegetable masters on various fronts.

The account utilizes key pacing to fabricate pressure as the hero's group blends, making way for the inescapable conflicts with Veggie Corp. Each partner's presentation turns into a story crescendo, increasing expectation for the cooperative endeavors that will characterize the obstruction's showdowns with the vegetable masters. The pacing permits perusers to observe the continuous development of a durable and imposing power.

The impossible partners' cooperations with Veggie Corp become a complicated dance of brains, methodologies, and counterstrategies. The account explores the nuanced elements of the obstruction's showdowns, depicting Veggie Corp's endeavors to sabotage the group's solidarity, exploit individual weaknesses, and kill their aggregate effect. The far-fetched partners, drawn from different areas of society, become tough safeguards against Veggie Corp's strategies, exemplifying the soul of obstruction and strength.

The peak of the story combines on the showdown between the far-fetched partners and Veggie Corp — a peak that rises above actual struggle and includes philosophical fighting, innovative duels, and social preparation. The different group turns into an image of aggregate opposition, testing the vegetable masters on numerous fronts. The story works to a crescendo, catching the force of the conflict and the extraordinary force of a unified, various front against settled in corporate strength.

The repercussions of the showdown investigates the results of the impossible partners' progress in testing Veggie Corp. The vegetable masters, once apparently strong, face public examination, lawful repercussions, and inner dispute. The story cautiously explores the fallout, recognizing both the victories and difficulties that go with the assorted group's endeavors to destroy the vegetable masters' impact.

3.3 Develop the relationships and dynamics within the team.

In the complex embroidery of "Green Conflicts: The Veggie Grudge," the connections and elements inside the hero's collected group structure a focal concentration, giving profundity and subtlety to the story. As this different gathering of people joins against Veggie Corp, the story digs into the developing associations, clashes, and shared encounters that characterize the group's excursion. This investigation unfurls the relational complexities, brotherhood, and difficulties looked by the characters as they explore the opposition against the vegetable masters.

The account cautiously lays out the underlying elements inside the group, underlining the variety of foundations, abilities, and inspirations. Every part brings an extraordinary point of view and skill, adding to the group's aggregate strength. The hero, going about as both pioneer and middle person, encourages a climate where singularity is commended, and each colleague's commitment is esteemed.

As the group frames, the story investigates the structure of trust and brotherhood among the different individuals. Shared encounters, whether in going up against Veggie Corp's harsh practices or conquering difficulties during missions, become the establishment for the bonds that integrate the group. The story illustrates the group as a very close unit, with every part perceiving the significance of fortitude in their battle against the shared adversary.

The hero's job as a pioneer is complex, enveloping vital direction, compromise, and the consistent encouragement important for a group confronting imposing chances. The account digs into the difficulties looked by the hero in adjusting the different characters inside the group, depicting the pioneer's capacity to explore conflicts, encourage solidarity, and move versatility.

Relational elements inside the group stretch out past expert cooperation, investigating the individual lives and chronicles of every part. The story dives into the singular accounts of the group, uncovering their inspirations for joining the obstruction and the individual penances they've made. These brief looks into their lives add layers to the characters, displaying the multidimensionality of their characters.

The connections inside the group are not without clashes, mirroring the innate difficulties of different characters pursuing a shared objective. The account explores snapshots of pressure, contrasting assessments on system, and periodic conflicts of self images. These struggles become open doors for character development, underscoring the significance of beating contrasts for everyone's benefit.

Heartfelt traps inside the group add a layer of intricacy to the story, entwining individual associations with the bigger setting of obstruction. The story investigates the sensitive harmony among individual and expert limits, recognizing the difficulties of exploring profound associations in the midst of the great stakes climate of their central goal. The heartfelt elements add to the account's investigation of human weakness and versatility notwithstanding difficulty.

The story meshes snapshots of levity and brotherhood into the group's excursion, giving snapshots of rest from the force of their main goal. Funny trades, shared triumphs, and holding exercises become basic parts of the story, displaying the strength of the human soul even amidst a wild fight against corporate authority. These snapshots of brotherhood highlight the significance of bliss and association as fundamental components of the obstruction.

As the group faces Veggie Corp's countermeasures, the story stresses the strength got from their solidarity. The vegetable masters endeavor to take advantage of fractures inside the group, utilizing individual weaknesses to plant disagreement. The opposition, notwithstanding, demonstrates tough even with such strategies, supporting the account's topic of aggregate strength and common perspective.

The account assembles pressure by presenting difficulties that test the group's attachment. High-stakes missions, unforeseen treacheries, and snapshots of moral equivocalness become cauldrons that force the group to face their qualities and the profundity of their obligation to the opposition. These difficulties move the characters into an excursion of self-revelation and aggregate development.

The developing elements inside the group are exhibited notwithstanding private misfortunes and difficulties. The account explores snapshots of sadness, featuring the group's capacity to help each other in the midst of distress. The characters' reactions to misfortune become critical in delineating the versatility of the group and their relentless assurance to own their main goal.

The hero's initiative style develops as the story advances, adjusting to the changing elements inside the group. The pioneer's capacity to gain from botches, pay attention to colleagues, and encourage a climate of shared regard becomes vital to the group's prosperity. The story depicts initiative not as a static job but rather as a dynamic, developing part of the hero's excursion.

As the group faces the climactic showdown with Veggie Corp, the account arrives at its apex, featuring the climax of the connections and elements created all through the story. The group's solidarity, fashioned through shared encounters and difficulties, turns into a considerable power that Veggie Corp battles to counter. The story works to a crescendo, catching the force of the group's aggregate obstruction against the vegetable masters.

The outcome of the showdown gives an intelligent space to the colleagues, permitting the story to investigate the effect of their process on each person. The bonds framed inside the group persevere, rising above the prompt mission against Veggie Corp. The story recognizes the enduring effect of the connections and elements created inside the group, depicting them as persevering through mainstays of flexibility notwithstanding progressing difficulties.

4

Chapter 4

The Quest for Forbidden Fruit

In the tragic scene of "Green Conflicts: The Veggie Quarrel," the story takes a convincing turn as the hero sets out on a hazardous mission for taboo natural product — a subtle wellspring of force and information that holds the way to testing Veggie Corp's domain. This investigation digs into the mission's beginnings, the hero's inspirations, the difficulties confronted, and the groundbreaking excursion that unfurls as they look to get the illegal products of the soil its true capacity against the vegetable masters.

The journey for illegal organic product is established in an enigmatic legend — a murmured story of a secret plantation that bears natural products immaculate by Veggie Corp's impact. This legendary plantation, disguised in the core of the taboo zones, turns into an image of opposition and an epitome of the expectation that humankind can recover command over its fate. The story cautiously unfurls the legend encompassing the illegal organic product, prodding the potential it holds and the dangers related with searching it out.

The hero's choice to leave on this journey is powered by a strong mix of distress, rebellion, and a hunger for information. As Veggie Corp's extremely tight grip on society fixes, the hero sees the prohibited organic product as the final opportunity to unwind the mysteries that could influence the situation for the opposition.

The mission turns into an individual odyssey, an excursion that rises above the quick battle against the vegetable masters and wanders into the domain of old secrets.

The story unpredictably investigates the hero's inspirations, diving into the profound scene that impels them into the dangerous mission. Maybe it's a firmly established craving for equity, a longing to retaliate for individual misfortunes, or a significant feeling of obligation to the people who have experienced under Veggie Corp's mistreatment. The mission for taboo natural product turns into an indication of the hero's internal conflict, an excursion driven by a perplexing interaction of distress, assurance, and a resolute feeling of direction.

The difficulties innate in the journey are complex, going from the actual dangers of exploring taboo zones to the scholarly riddles implanted in the legend of the legendary plantation. The story unfurls a progression of preliminaries that test the hero's flexibility, cleverness, and conviction. From sidestepping Veggie Corp's observation to translating enigmatic pieces of information that lead further into the prohibited zones, each challenge turns into a pot that changes the hero's personality.

The taboo zones, once lively and flourishing, have become barren scenes scarred by Veggie Corp's tenacious double-dealing. The story portrays the natural corruption created by the vegetable masters, under-lining the difference between the sterile monoculture forced by Veggie Corp and the wild, untamed excellence of the illegal zones. The mission for illegal natural product turns into an excursion through a world that bears the scars of uncontrolled corporate predominance.

As the hero adventures further into the taboo zones, the account presents puzzling characters who act as guides, gatekeepers, or impedi-ments on the mission. These characters might be remainders of a former time, rebels who opposed Veggie Corp's impact, or people who have tracked down comfort in the illegal zones' rebellion of the vegetable masters. Each experience adds layers to the account, uncovering parts of the illegal natural product's story and the more extensive history of obstruction against Veggie Corp.

The taboo natural product, when at last found, turns into an image of both information and power — an impetus for change. The story investigates the mysterious characteristics of the organic product, depicting it as a vault of old insight, stifled insights, and the possibility to upset Veggie Corp's control. The hero's cooperation with the taboo organic product turns into a critical second, denoting a change yet to be determined of force and a defining moment in the overall battle against the vegetable masters.

The story cautiously explores the results of getting the taboo organic product, both for the hero and the obstruction.

The freshly discovered information turns into a two sided deal, offering bits of knowledge into Veggie Corp's weaknesses and the necessary resources to counter their impact, yet in addition troubling the hero with the heaviness of obligation. The mission for taboo organic product changes from an actual excursion into a moral and vital test, as the hero wrestles with the moral ramifications of using such power.

The illegal natural product's true capacity is saddled as a weapon against Veggie Corp as well as a device for motivating expectation and preparing the opposition. The account investigates the hero's essential utilization of the illegal organic product's information, scattering data that excites the abused, uncovered Veggie Corp's wrongdoings, and sabotages the vegetable masters' painstakingly created exterior. The mission turns into an impetus for a more extensive uprising, as the obstruction unites behind the disclosure delivered by the taboo natural product.

The account interlaces the hero's very own excursion with the more extensive cultural effect of the journey for illegal organic product. As the opposition picks up speed, Veggie Corp answers with raising measures to stifle disagree. The taboo natural product turns into an image of opposition, testing the vegetable masters through face to face conflicts as well as by motivating an influx of grassroots developments, fights, and demonstrations of disobedience that reverberation across the tragic scene.

The hero's change all through the mission for prohibited natural product is a story circular segment in itself. The excursion, set apart by preliminaries and disclosures, turns into a pot that reshapes the hero's convictions, values, and comprehension of the world. The story explores snapshots of thoughtfulness, uncertainty, and self-disclosure, depicting the hero as a powerful person who develops because of the difficulties confronted and the information acquired.

The journey for illegal organic product comes full circle in a climactic showdown between the hero and Veggie Corp. The story works to a crescendo as the illegal information is released, uncovering the vegetable masters' most obscure insider facts and disentangling the groundworks of their control. The hero

's vital utilization of the prohibited organic product's disclosures turns into a weapon that penetrates through Veggie Corp's veneer, planting disagreement inside the partnership's positions and energizing help for the opposition.

The result of the mission for illegal natural product investigates the extensive outcomes of the hero's activities. Veggie Corp, when an unassailable power, faces inner dispute, public shock, and a developing opposition that rises above the limits of the taboo zones. The story cautiously explores the perplexing result, recognizing both the triumphs and difficulties that go with the hero's journey for taboo information.

4.1 Searching for a Legendary Artifact

In the sweeping story of "Green Conflicts: The Veggie Quarrel," a vital plotline unfurls as the hero leaves on a considering questing — looking for an unbelievable relic covered in legend and secret. This investigation dives into the beginnings of the antique's legend, the hero's inspirations for chasing after it, the difficulties looked during the mission, and the groundbreaking excursion that unfurls as they try to uncover the legendary article and saddle its true capacity against the considerable Veggie Corp.

The legend of the curio is profoundly imbued in the tragic legend of the story — a murmured story went down through ages, reverberating with both expectation and fear. This legendary item is said to have unrivaled abilities, fit for countering Veggie Corp's domain and reestablishing a similarity to adjust to the ruined world. The account cautiously winds around the strings of the ancient rarity's legend, stressing its mysterious nature and the wonderment it motivates among the people who set out to put stock in its presence.

The hero's choice to leave on the journey to find the unbelievable curio is catalyzed by an intense mix of urgency, rebellion, and a voracious hunger for change. As Veggie Corp's impact fixes its hold on each part of society, the curio turns into an image of opposition — an encouraging sign that guarantees an extraordinary power equipped for testing the vegetable masters. The mission, consequently, becomes an actual excursion as well as an otherworldly odyssey, driven by the hero's steadfast assurance to defy the harsh system.

The difficulties experienced during the mission for the incredible relic are diverse, each introducing a special preliminary that tests the hero's flexibility, resourcefulness, and commitment to the reason. From translating obscure signs concealed in old texts to exploring slippery landscapes immaculate by Veggie Corp's impact, the story unfurls a progression of preliminaries that shape the hero's personality and move them towards the core of the journey. The difficulties become soul changing experiences, changing the hero from a simple searcher into a considerable power against Veggie Corp.

The quest for the incredible ancient rarity takes the hero through taboo zones, neglected scenes that bear the scars of Veggie Corp's tenacious abuse. The story portrays these barren domains, differentiating the sterile monoculture forced by the vegetable masters with the wild, untamed excellence of the immaculate scenes. The mission turns into an excursion through a world that mirrors the division between the desolated present and the legendary past that holds the way to salvation.

The account presents puzzling characters along the way — gatekeepers, guides, or foes, each with their own association with the antique's legend. These characters might be remainders of opposition developments from former periods, researchers who have devoted their lives to disentangling the antique's secrets, or even Veggie Corp followers looking to smother any dangers to their domain. Each experience turns into an account turn, uncovering parts of the curio's story and the more extensive history of the people who have looked for it previously.

As the hero dives further into the mission, the account investigates the mental cost of the excursion. The persevering quest for the curio brings up issues of profound quality, reason, and the penances made for the sake of opposition. The hero wrestles with uncertainty, defying the moral intricacies of using such a strong article and the obligation it involves. The mission becomes an outer excursion as well as an inner investigation of the hero's convictions and the heaviness of their decisions.

The incredible relic, when at long last found, rises above simple rawness — it turns into a sign of force, insight, and the collected any desires for the individuals who looked for its legendary potential. The story dives into the hero's communication with the curio, depicting it as a snapshot of fellowship that rises above the material world. The relic turns into a channel for old information, a vault of failed to remember insights, and an impetus for the hero's change into a harbinger of progress.

The account explores the outcomes of getting the amazing antique, both for the hero and the overall obstruction against Veggie Corp. The recently discovered powers, while considerable, accompany a cost — the weight of employing a power that challenges the actual texture of the tragic culture. The relic's true capacity is tackled not just as an instrument for head-to-head a conflict with Veggie Corp yet in addition for the purpose of enlivening the mistreated masses, motivating expectation, and stirring a far reaching obstruction.

The hero's essential utilization of the incredible relic turns into a story point of convergence, unfurling a progression of conflicts between the opposition and Veggie Corp. The relic's powers upset Veggie Corp's control components, uncovering their wrongdoings, destroying their promulgation, and assembling the general population against their abusive system. The journey for the incredible relic changes from an individual odyssey into an impetus for cultural commotion — a story turn that pushes the opposition into a place of remarkable strength.

The repercussions of the mission gives an intelligent space to the hero and the opposition, permitting the story to investigate the more extensive effect of the incredible relic on the tragic world. Veggie Corp, when an unassailable power, faces inside cracks, outer difference, and a prospering opposition that will not be hushed. The story cautiously explores the repercussions, recognizing both the victories and difficulties that go with the hero's journey for the unbelievable curio.

4.2 The team embarks on a quest to find the forbidden fruit—a mysterious item rumored to have the power to counter Veggie Corp's influence.

In the grasping story of "Green Conflicts: The Veggie Grudge," the plot takes an arresting turn as the hero and their different group set out on a groundbreaking mission — a journey to track down the prohibited organic product, a baffling thing supposed to have the ability to counter Veggie Corp's severe impact. This investigation dives into the beginnings of the taboo organic product's legend, the inspirations driving the group's interest, the difficulties looked during their mission, and the significant excursion of self-revelation and obstruction that unfurls as they try to get this subtle and strong antiquity.

The legend of the taboo organic product is profoundly implanted in the tragic texture of the story — a story murmured among the persecuted, an encouraging sign in the midst of the unavoidable murkiness. The taboo organic product is said to hold onto special characteristics that can kill Veggie Corp's control, making it an image of obstruction and an impetus for change. The account carefully winds around the strings of this baffling legend, elevating its appeal and accentuating the feeling of secret and wonderment that encompasses the illegal natural product.

The group's choice to set out on the mission for the taboo organic product is catalyzed by an aggregate longing for freedom and a common assurance to challenge Veggie Corp's authority. The story digs into each colleague's very own inspirations, interlacing individual accounts of misfortune, unfairness, and a deep longing for a superior future. The journey turns into a common mission that rises above the individual, joining the group under a typical reason — to recover the taboo products of the soil its true capacity against the vegetable masters.

The difficulties looked by the group during the mission for the taboo organic product are complex, going from actual dangers to scholarly riddles profoundly laced with the legend. The story unfurls a progression of preliminaries that test the group's union, genius, and versatility. Exploring prohibited zones, translating old texts, and outmaneuvering Veggie Corp's observation become soul changing experiences that change the group from a dissimilar gathering into a bound together power of obstruction.

The taboo zones, when flourishing environments, are portrayed as forsaken scenes scarred by Veggie Corp's constant double-dealing. The story paints a clear differentiation between the sterile monoculture forced by the vegetable masters and the untamed excellence of the prohibited zones. The mission turns into an excursion through the leftovers of a world that has experienced under corporate predominance, stressing the group's disobedience as they track upon these prohibited domains.

Puzzling characters experienced during the mission add layers to the story, filling in as guides, watchmen, or foes. These characters might be remainders of opposition developments, managers of old information, or people who have endured straightforwardly under Veggie Corp's standard. Each experience turns into an account turn, uncovering parts of the prohibited organic product's story and giving bits of knowledge into the more extensive history of opposition against the vegetable masters.

As the group dives further into the mission, the account investigates the mental cost of the excursion. Uncertainty, dread, and the heaviness of obligation weigh vigorously in each colleague. The story explores the unseen conflicts as the group wrestles with the moral ramifications of looking for a power that might actually reshape the equilibrium of their reality. The mission becomes an outside campaign as well as an inside investigation of the group's convictions and their obligation to the more prominent reason.

The illegal organic product, when at last found, turns into a point of convergence of the story — an image of trust, strengthening, and resistance. The story unpredictably investigates the group's connection with the prohibited organic product, depicting it as a snapshot of disclosure that rises above the actual domain. The taboo natural product turns into a channel for old insight, a wellspring of obstruction, and an impetus for the group's development into considerable challengers against Veggie Corp.

The results of acquiring the taboo organic product are both significant and complex. The story explores the freshly discovered powers and information, depicting them as a blade that cuts both ways. The group's essential utilization of the taboo organic product turns into a story curve in itself, trying Veggie Corp's predominance on different fronts. The prohibited natural product turns into a device for uncovering Veggie Corp's wrongdoings, energizing the mistreated, and moving a rush of dispute that fans out like quickly.

The account entwines snapshots of win and penance as the group utilizes the prohibited organic product's powers in their showdowns with Veggie Corp. The vegetable masters, once apparently invulnerable, face inner contradiction, outside disobedience, and a developing obstruction filled by the illegal organic product's disclosures. The journey turns into a defining moment in the overall battle against Veggie Corp, representing the group's assurance to oppose persecution and recover organization.

The consequence of the mission gives an intelligent space to the group, permitting the story to investigate the more extensive effect of their activities. Veggie Corp, confronted with the disclosure delivered by the prohibited natural product, defies inside breaks, public shock, and a disintegrating veneer of strength. The story cautiously explores the outcome, recognizing both the victories and difficulties that go with the group's endeavors to tackle the prohibited organic product's true capacity.

4.3 Along the way, they face various challenges and encounters with vegetable enforcers.

In the exciting adventure of "Green Conflicts: The Veggie Feud," the group's mission for the prohibited natural product unfurls as an unsafe excursion loaded up with difficulties and experiences with Veggie Corp's imposing masters. This story investigation digs into the hindrances thronw along their way, the persistent pursuit by vegetable implementers, and the group's aggregate versatility as they explore the slippery landscape in their quest for the subtle illegal natural product.

The group's process is set apart by a progression of difficulties, each intended to test their fortitude and assurance. As they cross illegal zones, when energetic scenes presently defaced by Veggie Corp's double-dealing, the story portrays the natural corruption created by the vegetable masters. The destruction turns into an impression of the difficulties looked by the group, representing the size of their mission to resist the harsh system.

Exploring these taboo zones requires the group to face actual hindrances as well as mysterious riddles and antiquated puzzles entwined with the legend of the illegal natural product. The story unfurls an embroidery of preliminaries, going from interpreting perplexing images to outmaneuvering Veggie Corp's reconnaissance instruments. Each challenge turns into a pot that fashions the group's solidarity, improving their aggregate abilities and cleverness.

As the group advances, the story presents Veggie Corp's persevering masters — enthusiastic protectors of the vegetable masters' territory. These masters, whether increased with vegetable innovation or inculcated into an obsessive faithfulness, become imposing enemies, epitomizing the actual pith of Veggie Corp's severe may. The experiences with these implementers add a layer of force to the story, increasing the stakes of the group's mission.

The vegetable implementers, clad in the sterile consistency forced by Veggie Corp, act as the actual sign of the company's dictator control. The story investigates their relentless dedication, their high level innovative improvements, and their enduring obligation to suppress any obstruction. The implementers become the exemplification of Veggie Corp's countermeasures, a still up in the air to defeat the group's mission for the prohibited organic product.

The showdowns with the vegetable masters become story crescendos, minutes where the group's solidarity and individual qualities are put to a definitive test. The masters, outfitted with vegetable-implanted advancements and inculcated philosophies, become imposing adversaries, compelling the group to utilize shrewd systems, exploit shortcomings, and feature their developing abilities. Each experience turns into a heartbeat beating episode, highlighting the group's strength even with overpowering chances.

The story cautiously explores the mental cost of the group's steady conflicts with Veggie Corp's implementers. The always present danger, the vulnerability of endurance, and the heaviness of the illegal organic product's importance make an environment of consistent strain. The colleagues, each wrestling with their own feelings of trepidation and questions, track down comfort and strength in their mutual perspective — a reason that reaches out past private inspirations to the aggregate longing for opportunity.

The experiences with vegetable implementers act as snapshots of character advancement, displaying the group's development, flexibility, and steadfast responsibility. Every triumph, whether hard-battled or vital, turns into a demonstration of their aggregate ability despite Veggie Corp's severe apparatus. The story meshes these snapshots of win into the more extensive embroidery of the group's excursion, underscoring the groundbreaking idea of their journey for the prohibited organic product.

The pursuit by Veggie Corp's masters turns into a persevering pursue, raising the story's pressure and driving the group into a high-stakes waiting game. The prohibited zones, when a shelter from Veggie Corp's impact, change into milestones where the group should continually outsmart and outmaneuver their followers. The story uses pacing to intensify the need to get moving, making a powerful rhythmic movement as the group explores the consistently developing difficulties.

In the midst of the pursuit, the account presents snapshots of reprieve and key preparation. The group, using their different abilities and foundations, plans on the best way to outmaneuver Veggie Corp's masters, interpret mysterious signs, and defeat the following arrangement of hindrances. These intervals become story breaths, permitting perusers to dive into the complexities of the group's elements, exhibiting their brotherhood and aggregate critical thinking ability.

As the group inches nearer to the taboo natural product, the story works towards a climactic showdown with Veggie Corp's most considerable implementer — a high-positioning specialist furnished with state of the art vegetable innovation and relentless devotion to the organization. The standoff turns into a summit of the group's excursion, a second where their flexibility, solidarity, and vital discernment are put to a definitive test.

The fallout of the climactic showdown gives an intelligent delay in the story, permitting the group to survey the cost of their experiences with Veggie Corp's implementers. The scars, both physical and close to home, become unmistakable tokens of the difficulties confronted and the penances made in their quest for the prohibited organic product. The account cautiously explores this result, recognizing the group's victories and misfortunes, and making way for the last leg of their groundbreaking process.

Chapter 5

Undercover Operations

In the tragic scene of "Green Conflicts: The Veggie Quarrel," the story takes an arresting turn as the group participates in a progression of covert tasks — perplexing missions intended to penetrate Veggie Corp's internal sanctums, accumulate knowledge, and strike at the core of the vegetable masters' strength. This investigation digs into the beginnings of the secret tasks, the inspirations driving the group to go covert, the difficulties looked in keeping up with mystery, and the unfurling adventure of undercover work and opposition that follows.

The choice to set out on covert activities originates from the group's acknowledgment of the requirement for key disruption. Veggie Corp, with its inescapable impact, firmly controls data stream and screens any contradiction with savage proficiency. The account complicatedly meshes the thought processes of each colleague into the aggregate choice to dive into the shadows, featuring the longing to uncover Veggie Corp's secret maneuvers and take advantage of the chinks in their apparently impervious protective layer.

The secret tasks require an extreme change in the group's methodology, from plain rebellion to nuance and vital artfulness. The story illustrates the preparation and arrangement expected for every activity, underlining the group's fastidious thought of masks, bogus characters, and incognito specialized strategies. The individuals, each offering a special arrangement of abilities of real value, become specialists of disruption, exploring the confounded passages of Veggie Corp's impact with tact and tricky.

The difficulties innate in covert tasks are complex, going from the steady danger of revelation to the mental cost of keeping an exterior even with Veggie Corp's teaching. The story unfurls a progression of tense minutes as the colleagues explore corporate occasions, secret gatherings, and surreptitious spaces, consistently on the incline of openness. The tension becomes tangible, complemented by the consistently present gamble of selling out and the heaviness of the illegal information they convey.

Veggie Corp's authorities, watchful and heartless, become imposing foes in the secret activities. The story acquaints the group with a trap of observation, infiltrators, and counterintelligence estimates that Veggie Corp utilizes to suppress disagree. Every activity turns into a high-stakes mental contest, with the colleagues handily dodging recognition while crawling nearer to the core of Veggie Corp's dim mysteries.

The mental cost of living under the consistent danger of revelation turns into a story point of convergence, diving into the cost it takes in the group's psychological and profound prosperity. The spies wrestle with the duality of their reality — exploring Veggie Corp's reality by day while plotting its defeat around evening time. The account cautiously explores the unseen struggles, distrustfulness, and snapshots of self-question that go with the covert tasks, adding layers of intricacy to the characters' encounters.

The account decisively reveals the inward operations of Veggie Corp through the eyes of the covert group. Corporate meeting rooms, shadowy labs, and covert gatherings become the setting against which the group uncovers the company's haziest insider facts. The story winds around an embroidery of interest and disclosure, displaying Veggie

Corp's control of data, double-dealing of assets, and the slippery manners by which they keep up with command over the tragic culture.

As the group accesses Veggie Corp's inward sanctums, the account investigates the ethical issues looked by the spies. The illegal information they gain, while significant for the opposition, turns into a load on their heart. The story explores snapshots of moral situation, underlining the unseen conflicts as the group wrestles with the line between important disruption and the potential moral trade off inborn in their secret jobs.

Heartfelt entrapments inside the secret tasks add a layer of intricacy to the story, interlacing individual associations with the more extensive background of obstruction. The story investigates the fragile harmony between adoration, devotion, and the current mission, recognizing the difficulties of keeping up with close to home associations amidst a high-stakes undercover work game. The heartfelt elements become vital to the account's investigation of weakness and versatility despite Veggie Corp's abusive system.

The story meshes snapshots of strain and delivery into the covert tasks, making a unique cadence that keeps perusers as eager and anxious as ever. High-stakes missions, near disasters, and startling collusions become story turns, driving the story forward and working towards a climactic disclosure. The pressure turns into a story gadget, elevating the effect of each diversion in the secret tasks.

As the covert tasks unfurl, the account investigates the advancing elements inside the group. The common insider facts, the steady danger of openness, and the shared reliance on each other make a remarkable brotherhood among the spies. The story digs into the bonds produced in the cauldron of mystery, featuring the group's versatility and the groundbreaking force of mutual perspective.

The peak of the secret tasks turns into a story pinnacle, a second where the group's clandestine endeavors merge with the more extensive obstruction against Veggie Corp. The illegal information gained through reconnaissance turns into an impetus for an organized uprising, uncovering Veggie Corp's wrongdoings, preparing the mistreated masses, and testing the actual underpinnings of the vegetable masters' control.

The consequence of the secret tasks gives an intelligent space to the group, permitting the story to investigate the effect of their undercover work endeavors on both Veggie Corp and the obstruction. The disclosures uncovered by the spies become a powerful weapon, undermining Veggie Corp's position and moving a flood of dispute that resounds across the tragic scene. The story cautiously explores the outcomes, recognizing the triumphs and forfeits that go with the group's thinking for even a second to introduction to the core of Veggie Corp's domain.

5.1 Infiltrating Veggie Corp

In the vivid story of "Green Conflicts: The Veggie Feud," a urgent part unfurls as the group tries to penetrate the core of Veggie Corp — a trying and high-stakes mission that fills in as the peak of their obstruction against the vegetable masters.

This investigation dives into the inspirations impelling the group to embrace such a hazardous undertaking, the complexities of the penetration plan, the difficulties experienced inside the strengthened walls of Veggie Corp, and the unfurling adventure of trickery, disclosure, and resistance that characterizes this groundbreaking story bend.

The choice to penetrate Veggie Corp rises out of an aggregate acknowledgment of the need to strike at the focal point of the harsh system. The account complicatedly winds around together the singular inspirations of each colleague, their own stakes in the obstruction, and the common assurance to uncover Veggie Corp's most strictly confidential mysteries. The mission turns into an emblematic and key summit of the group's endeavors, a thinking for even a second to wander into the place of extreme peril to uncover the defilement at its center.

The preparation and groundwork for the invasion unfurl as a fastidious dance of system and deception. The story portrays the group's secretive activities, itemizing the production of bogus characters, the acquisition of Veggie Corp garbs, and the cautious investigation of the organization's security conventions. The colleagues, each carrying their exceptional abilities to the front, become modelers of an intricate arrangement that requires impeccable execution to penetrate Veggie Corp's considerable safeguards.

The difficulties inborn in penetrating Veggie Corp are stupendous, going from sidestepping best in class observation frameworks to exploring twisted corporate designs intended to repulse gatecrashers. The story unfurls a progression of snags that test the group's spryness, inventiveness, and aggregate flexibility. The actual substance of Veggie Corp's predominance lies in its capacity to control data, and entering these layers turns into a story cauldron that characterizes the group's strength.

As the group penetrates the external safeguards, the account dives into the fastidiously built veneer of Veggie Corp's corporate ideal world. Meeting rooms enhanced with smooth vegetable-enlivened feel, immaculate labs leading slippery analyses, and the clean passages where authorities watch become the background against which the group disentangles the company's haziest privileged insights. The invasion turns into an excursion into the core of the tragic hardware, uncovering the guileful underside that lies underneath the surface.

Veggie Corp's masters, cautious and tenacious, represent an impressive test inside the company's walls. The story acquaints the group with an elevated condition of reconnaissance, upgraded safety efforts, and the consistently present gamble of location. Each experience with masters turns into a heartbeat beating second, stressing the razor-slight edge among progress and disappointment. The strain ascends as the group moves through the corporate maze, evading the full concentrations eyes of those faithful to the vegetable masters.

The account decisively uncovers the layers of mystery inside Veggie Corp, exhibiting the organization's control of data, double-dealing of assets, and the degree to which it controls the story of the tragic culture. The group's invasion turns into a story gadget for uncovering Veggie Corp's wrongdoings, pulling back the shade on the company's painstakingly created exterior. The illegal information procured inside Veggie

Corp's internal sanctums turns into a weapon that might possibly break the underpinnings of the severe system.

The mental cost of living covert inside Veggie Corp's walls turns into a story point of convergence. The colleagues, shrouded in misdirection, wrestle with the duality of their reality — exploring corporate capabilities and keeping up with their cover while plotting the enterprise's ruin in the shadows. The account digs into the unseen fits of turmoil, distrustfulness, and snapshots of self-question that go with the group's invasion, adding layers of intricacy to their characters and encounters.

In the midst of the penetration, the story presents snapshots of startling coalitions and disclosures. The group, moving like ghosts inside Veggie Corp, finds pockets of contradiction and people thoughtful to the opposition cause. These partners inside the company become account impetuses, offering pivotal data, working with incognito developments, and adding a component of unconventionality to the group's main goal. The story investigates the fragile dance of trust and disruption inside Veggie Corp's walls, displaying the versatility of the human soul even in the most harsh conditions.

The story musically works towards climactic minutes inside Veggie Corp — a progression of experiences, disclosures, and disclosures that come full circle in a showdown with the partnership's most elevated echelons. The invasion turns into a story crescendo, a second where the group's secret endeavors converge with the more extensive obstruction against Veggie Corp. The illegal information procured inside the company's walls turns into the key part for an organized uprising, a disclosure that electrifies the persecuted masses and difficulties Veggie Corp's extremely tight grip on society.

The result of the invasion gives an intelligent space to the group, permitting the story to investigate the effect of their trying mission on both Veggie Corp and the obstruction. The disclosures exposed by the infiltrators become an impetus for boundless contradiction, starting fights, uprisings, and a groundswell of opposition that resounds across the tragic scene. The story cautiously explores the results, recognizing the victories and penances that go with the group's brassy introduction to the core of Veggie Corp.

5.2 The team devises a plan to infiltrate Veggie Corp's head-quarters.

In the unfurling story of "Green Conflicts: The Veggie Grudge," a critical crossroads arises as the group, energized by an aggregate assurance to disentangle the secrets of Veggie Corp and break its harsh territory, fastidiously devises an arrangement to penetrate the actual heart of the vegetable masters' realm — Veggie Corp's impressive base camp. This investigation dives into the inspirations that drive the group towards such a risky endeavor, the perplexing subtleties of the penetration plan, the difficulties that intersperse their incognito excursion, and the extraordinary adventure that results inside the invigorated walls of Veggie Corp.

The choice to invade Veggie Corp's central command isn't conceived out of foolishness yet rather from a level-headed affirmation of the need to strike at the focal point of the severe system. The story complicatedly winds around together the singular inspirations of each colleague, entwining individual stakes, past complaints, and a common obligation to free society from Veggie Corp's shackles. The mission becomes meaningful — a really considering trying to face the actual focal point of debasement and divulge the mysteries that have kept Veggie Corp in power.

The arranging stage unfurls as an orchestra of mind and shrewd technique. The story portrays the group crouched together, their different ranges of abilities uniting into an amicable mix of mastery. Making bogus characters, concentrating on Veggie Corp's security framework, and unraveling the overly complex design of the central command become significant components in the arrangement. The group, presently like never before, embodies an undercover power ready to challenge the impervious fortification of Veggie Corp.

The difficulties intrinsic in penetrating Veggie Corp's base camp are stupendous, mirroring the extent of their bold mission. The story unfurls a progression of impediments, each testing the group's spryness, creativity, and cooperative versatility. Dodging cutting edge observation frameworks, outfoxing careful masters, and exploring the unpredictable halls of the corporate fortress become account cauldrons that produce the group's grit and assurance.

As the group penetrates the external safeguards, the account dives into the lofty and forcing veneer of Veggie Corp's base camp. Meeting rooms embellished with clean loftiness, labs leading furtive investigations, and the clean passageways where authorities watch become the material against which the group unwinds the enterprise's most obscure insider facts. The invasion turns into an excursion into the actual stomach of the tragic monster, a journey to uncover the secret intrigues that drive Veggie Corp's severe system.

Veggie Corp's implementers, watchful and immovable, act as imposing enemies inside the enterprise's walls. The story acquaints the group with an increased condition of observation, high level safety efforts, and the steady gamble of discovery. Each experience with implementers turns into a snapshot of strain, a sensitive dance on the cliff of openness. The story ably uplifts the stakes, accentuating the always present risk that weaving machines the group moves through the passageways of force.

The account decisively divulges the layers of mystery inside Veggie Corp, giving looks into the partnership's control of data, double-dealing of assets, and the degree to which it controls the story of the tragic culture. The group's invasion turns into a story instrument for uncovering Veggie Corp's offenses, pulling back the drapery on the partnership's painstakingly created exterior. The taboo information gained inside Veggie Corp's internal sanctums turns into a weapon that can possibly destroy the actual underpinnings of the severe system.

The mental cost of living covert inside Veggie Corp's central command turns into a story point of convergence. The colleagues, wrapped in duplicity, wrestle with the duality of their reality — exploring corporate capabilities and keeping up with their cover while plotting the partnership's ruin in the shadows. The story dives into the struggles under the surface, the distrustfulness, and the snapshots of self-question that go with the group's invasion, adding layers of intricacy to their characters and encounters.

Inside Veggie Corp's walls, the story presents snapshots of surprising coalitions and disclosures. The group, moving like ghosts inside the core of the enterprise, finds pockets of contradiction and people thoughtful to the opposition cause. These partners inside the central command become account impetuses, offering critical data, working with incognito developments, and infusing a component of unusualness into the group's main goal. The account investigates the sensitive dance of trust and disruption inside Veggie Corp's impressive walls, exhibiting the versatility of the human soul even in the most severe conditions.

The story musically works towards climactic minutes inside Veggie Corp — a progression of experiences, disclosures, and disclosures that finish in a showdown with the company's most elevated echelons. The invasion turns into a story crescendo, a second where the group's incognito endeavors meet with the more extensive opposition against Veggie Corp. The taboo information gained inside the company's walls turns into the key part for an organized uprising — a disclosure that electrifies the mistreated masses and difficulties Veggie Corp's extremely tight grip on society.

The fallout of the invasion gives an intelligent space to the group, permitting the story to investigate the effect of their trying mission on both Veggie Corp and the opposition.

The disclosures uncovered by the infiltrators become an impetus for inescapable dispute, starting fights, uprisings, and a groundswell of opposition that resonates across the tragic scene. The account cautiously explores the results, recognizing the victories and penances that go with the group's bold introduction to the core of Veggie Corp.

5.3 Uncover Veggie Corp's nefarious plans and the true extent of their control.

In the vivid story of "Green Conflicts: The Veggie Quarrel," the group's daring penetration into Veggie Corp's central command turns into the channel for divulging the company's detestable plans and uncovering the genuine degree of their command over the tragic culture. This investigation dives into the disclosures that arise as the group digs further into the internal sanctums of Veggie Corp, the evil plots exposed, and the significant ramifications that reshape the scene of opposition against the vegetable masters.

As the group explores the complex hallways of Veggie Corp's base camp, the story complicatedly strips back the layers of mystery covering the organization's actual goals. Meeting rooms and research centers once hid behind an impeccable façade now uncover the slippery plans Veggie Corp has brought forth to fix its grasp on power. The story turns into a channel for prohibited information, disentangling a snare of control, double-dealing, and control that reaches out a long ways past what the group had at first imagined.

Veggie Corp's evil plans become known as the group accesses ordered records, snoops on undercover discussions, and interprets scrambled documents inside the partnership's gotten servers. The story portrays Veggie Corp's plan — a carefully created procedure to additionally oppress the majority, exploit regular assets extremely close to consumption, and cement their strength over each feature of society. The group turns into the caretaker of a stash of dooming proof that discloses the enterprise's noxious plans.

Inside the research centers disguised inside Veggie Corp's base camp, the story discloses the degree of the company's innovative progressions — an evil combination of vegetable-imbued advances pointed toward expanding their control. The examinations directed inside these mystery chambers uncover the dull underside of Veggie Corp's quest for power, with vegetable-based upgrades intended to control minds, uphold consistence, and stifle any similarity to opposition. The story cautiously explores the ethical ramifications of such logical undertakings, featuring the moral problems looked by the group as they reveal Veggie Corp's noxious examinations.

The control applied by Veggie Corp reaches out past actual strength, diving into the control of data and insight. The account investigates the partnership's dominance in forming stories, spreading promulgation, and controlling the shared perspective of the tragic culture. The group coincidentally finds huge organizations of disinformation, painstakingly created to keep up with Veggie Corp's kindhearted veneer while stifling any disagreeing voices. The story turns into a reflection on the force of data and the difficulties of exploring an existence where truth is an intriguing item.

The genuine degree of Veggie Corp's control is additionally highlighted by the group's revelation of the organization's financial extremely tight grip. The story strips back the layers of corporate intrigues, uncovering a monopolistic command over assets, exchange, and trade. Veggie Corp's monetary control turns into a weapon of mass enslavement, driving the general population into reliance and guaranteeing their consistence through financial pressure. The group turns out to be keenly conscious that difficult Veggie Corp's predominance requires uncovering their pernicious plans as well as destroying the financial shackles that tight spot society.

The account explores the group's personal and mental reaction to the stunning disclosures. The heaviness of the prohibited information, the ethical weight of seeing Veggie Corp's abominations, and the acknowledgment that their general public has been efficiently mistreated become impactful minutes in the account. The colleagues, each wrestling with their own ethical compass, stand up to the cruel truth that the fight against Veggie Corp isn't just physical yet in addition a battle for hearts and brains.

Veggie Corp's command over the political scene turns into a point of convergence of the story, with the group uncovering the organization's puppetry in the most elevated echelons of government. The story uncovered a trap of defilement, pressure, and control that reaches out to the most elevated workplaces, delivering the political hardware docile to Veggie Corp's impulses. The group's penetration uncovers a general public caught in a political act, where the deception of a vote based system veils the imperious rule of vegetable masters.

The real essence of Veggie Corp's desires rises above the bounds of a simple corporate substance. The story divulges the enterprise's self important arrangement for worldwide predominance, with ringlets stretching out past public boundaries. Veggie Corp's impact is depicted as a metastasizing force, penetrating legislatures, economies, and societies around the world. The group's disclosure turns into a disclosure of worldwide extents, featuring the interconnectedness of Veggie Corp's grasp on power and the greatness of the obstruction expected to liberate the world from its grip.

As the group wrestles with the hugeness of Veggie Corp's control, the account shifts towards the ramifications for the more extensive obstruction development. The taboo information turns into a two sided deal, enabling the group with the bits of knowledge expected to plan against Veggie Corp yet in addition troubling them with the obligation of exciting a divided and persecuted society. The story cautiously investigates the sensitive harmony between utilizing reality as a weapon and defending against the potential confusion that might result.

The story musically works towards a peak where the group should choose how to use the information they've uncovered. The illegal disclosures become a mobilizing weep for the mistreated, an invitation to battle against Veggie Corp's oppression. The group, presently infiltrators as well as modelers of opposition, wrestles with the essential ramifications of their newly discovered information. The story turns into a concentrate in administration, strength, and the extraordinary force of truth even with a treacherous foe.

Chapter 6

The Battle for Veggie Supremacy

In the climactic account curve of "Green Conflicts: The Veggie Quarrel," the stage is set for the clash that would blow anyone's mind — the Fight for Veggie Matchless quality. This vital section unfurls as the group, furnished with prohibited information and electrifies by the disclosures of Veggie Corp's harsh control, drives an unfaltering obstruction against the vegetable masters. This investigation dives into the essential development to the fight, the persevering conflicts that characterize the contention, the individual stakes of the characters, and the extraordinary peak that shapes the fate of the tragic world.

As the group rises out of the shadows of Veggie Corp's central command, their invasion fills in as the impetus for an essential development towards a definitive standoff — the Fight for Veggie Matchless quality. The prohibited information they convey turns into a mobilizing sob for the mistreated masses, motivating a groundswell of difference that combines into a bound together obstruction. The story catches the energy of a general public arousing to reality, throwing away the cloak of obliviousness, and embracing the call to challenge Veggie Corp's oppression.

The essential development envelops a progression of covert gatherings, underground social events, and the dispersal of data obtained during the group's penetration. The story unpredictably winds around the strategic parts of obstruction — the enlistment of different groups, the pooling of assets, and the essential arranging expected to mount a believable test to Veggie Corp's matchless quality. The group advances from infiltrators to engineers of defiance, fashioning partnerships and situating themselves as the vanguard of the opposition development.

The milestone for Veggie Incomparability is painstakingly picked — a representative union of Veggie Corp's transcending central command and the mistreated masses longing for freedom. The story clearly lays out the scene — the corporate fortification, its sterile designs compared against the natural disorder of a general public defying vegetable masters. The setting turns into a visual representation, mirroring the polarity between the mechanical unbending nature of Veggie Corp's control and the untamed soul of the obstruction.

The conflicts that characterize the Fight for Veggie Incomparability are persevering and extreme, mirroring the size of the contention. The account arranges scenes of engagements, vital moves, and the conflict of belief systems on the combat zone. Veggie Corp's masters, expanded with vegetable-imbued advancements, become impressive rivals, their steadfastness to the vegetable masters clear in their enduring obligation to subduing the disobedience. The account investigates the instinctive idea of battle, increasing the stakes with each conflict and highlighting the sheer assurance of the individuals who have ascended against abuse.

The group, presently at the very front of the opposition, wrestles with the individual stakes of the fight. The account dives into the subtle conflicts of each person — inspirations, fears, and the heaviness of administration. The heroes, roused by a feeling of equity and individual feuds against Veggie Corp, defy the hugeness of their parts in driving a disobedience. The individual stories interlace with the more extensive embroidery of the fight, making a rich profound scene that resounds with perusers.

Veggie Corp, understanding the existential danger presented by the disobedience, conveys its most cutting edge innovations and masters to smother the uprising. The story unfurls a progression of conflicts that act as heartbeat beating crescendos — minutes where the group's solidarity, technique, and versatility are put to a definitive test. The fights become microcosms of the bigger battle for Veggie Matchless quality, each conflict repeating the more extensive account of opposition against an abusive system.

The story musically shifts back and forth between the great scene of the war zone and personal minutes that investigate the characters' development and change. The individual accounts of penance, kinship, and the cost of the fight become vital strings woven into the texture of the overall story. The characters, manufactured in the cauldron of contention, develop into images of rebellion, typifying the aggregate soul of the obstruction.

The Fight for Veggie Incomparability isn't only an actual showdown however a conflict of belief systems. The story investigates the philosophical underpinnings of Veggie Corp's predominance — their vision of a world constrained by vegetables and the apparent need of enslaving humankind for everyone's benefit. The opposition, conversely, encapsulates the standards of opportunity, uniqueness, and the dismissal of a forced vegetable pecking order. The conflict of these restricting belief systems turns into a story investigation of the inborn battle between tyrant control and the human longing for independence.

The story works towards an extraordinary peak — a second where the tide of the fight remains in a critical state, and the destiny of Veggie Matchless still up in the air. The group, presently fight solidified heads of the disobedience, faces Veggie Corp's charming chief — a person who exemplifies the company's belief system not entirely set in stone to suppress the obstruction. The showdown turns into a representative battle, a standoff that typifies the more extensive struggle between Veggie Corp and the powers of freedom.

In the peak, the story investigates the individual inspirations of Veggie Corp's chief, disentangling the layers of their convictions, desires, and the base of their devotion to vegetables. The magnetic pioneer turns into a perplexing bad guy, and the story digs into their mind, refining them all the while. This investigation adds profundity to the story, testing the oversimplified division of good clashing with evil and highlighting the intricacy of the battle for Veggie Incomparability.

The groundbreaking peak unfurls as a crescendo of disclosures, penances, and the climax of the characters' circular segments. The story cautiously explores the profound reverberation of key minutes — the victories, misfortunes, and the cost of rebellion. The fight turns into a cauldron that manufactures the destiny of Veggie Matchless quality as well as the development of the characters who have embraced this burdensome excursion. The story underscores the unstoppable soul of the human will, the limit with regards to change, and the persevering through force of aggregate obstruction.

As the residue chooses the combat zone, the story enters an intelligent outcome — a space to investigate the fallout of the Fight for Veggie Matchless quality. The scene is changed, both genuinely and philosophically. Veggie Corp's control is broken, and the story catches the principal breaths of a general public freed from the severe system. The individual accounts of the characters end up back at square one, offering conclusion to their singular circular segments while laying the basis for the rise of another request.

6.1 Showdown at Veggie Corp HQ

In the arresting story of "Green Conflicts: The Veggie Feud," the climactic part unfurls with the Standoff at Veggie Corp HQ — a pivotal showdown that fills in as the peak of the opposition's battle against the vegetable masters. This investigation digs into the essential development prompting the standoff, the individual stakes of the characters in question, the overly complex difficulties looked inside Veggie Corp's base camp, and the extraordinary peak that reclassifies the fate of the tragic world.

The essential development towards the Standoff at Veggie Corp HQ is an ensemble of strain and expectation. The story explores the fallout of the Fight for Veggie Matchless quality, where the obstruction has managed a critical disaster for Veggie Corp's predominance. The enduring implementers of the vegetable masters retreat to the strengthened central command, and the stage is set for the last a conflict. The obstruction, floated by their new victories, solidifies their powers and figures out how to penetrate the last stronghold of Veggie Corp's control.

As the opposition merges on Veggie Corp HQ, the story portrays the corporate fortress — a rambling complex of smooth, forcing structures encompassed by intensely strengthened walls. The base camp stands as a demonstration of Veggie Corp's innovative ability and dictator control. The story catches the visual polarity between the sterile greatness of the partnership's fortress and the ragtag gathering not entirely set in stone to challenge its strength.

The characters, presently prepared heads of the opposition, wrestle with the individual stakes of the standoff. The account dives into the close to home and mental consequence of the Fight for Veggie Incomparability, investigating the scars, misfortunes, and the unflinching assurance that drives the heroes forward. Each person, formed by their singular processes, combines towards Veggie Corp HQ with a significant feeling of direction, their inspirations interlacing with the more extensive story of freedom.

The arrangement to invade Veggie Corp HQ turns into a story point of convergence, requiring a sensitive equilibrium of system, deception, and aggregate flexibility.

The story discloses the complexities of the obstruction's arrangement — producing partnerships with groups thoughtful to their objective, taking advantage of shortcomings in Veggie Corp's protections, and utilizing the taboo information obtained during the penetration. The stakes are higher than any time in recent memory, and the progress of the arrangement relies on the characters' capacity to outmaneuver

Veggie Corp's excess masters and explore the overly complex difficulties inside the sustained walls.

The difficulties inside Veggie Corp HQ are multi-layered, mirroring the partnership's assurance to save its domain. The story unfurls a progression of hindrances that test the opposition's guts — the observation frameworks, traps, and faithful implementers who stay immovable in their devotion to the vegetable masters. Each step towards the internal sanctums of Veggie Corp turns into a story pot, underscoring the creativity, versatility, and aggregate inventiveness of the opposition.

The account decisively uncovers the inward activities of Veggie Corp HQ, displaying the enterprise's final desperate attempts to keep up with control. Labs directing tricky analyses, publicity hardware dispersing disinformation, and the headquarters where Veggie Corp's charming chief organizes the last safeguard — all become story components that uplift the stakes and highlight the tremendousness of the obstruction's errand. The heroes become pioneers inside a tragic maze, unwinding the privileged insights that have supported Veggie Corp's persecution.

Veggie Corp's authorities, presently sustained inside the last stronghold of the company's control, arise as considerable enemies. The story presents an uplifted condition of reconnaissance, high level safety efforts, and the consistently present gamble of recognition. Each experience with implementers turns into a heartbeat beating second, stressing the razor-meager edge among progress and disappointment. The pressure ascends as the opposition moves through the corporate maze, evading the full concentrations eyes of those faithful to the vegetable masters.

The story explores the mental cost of penetrating Veggie Corp HQ — a space where the characters should wrestle with the steady danger of revelation, the heaviness of their central goal, and the information that the destiny of the opposition relies on their prosperity. The internal struggles, distrustfulness, and snapshots of self-question become account gadgets that add layers of intricacy to the characters and uplift the tension of the standoff.

In the midst of the difficulties inside Veggie Corp HQ, the story presents unforeseen partners and disclosures. The obstruction finds pockets of dispute inside the enterprise — people frustrated by Veggie Corp's oppression and ready to help the defiance.

These partners inside the base camp become account impetuses, offering urgent data, working with clandestine developments, and infusing a component of eccentricism into the standoff. The story investigates the sensitive dance of trust and disruption inside Veggie Corp's imposing walls, exhibiting the flexibility of the human soul even in the most harsh conditions.

As the obstruction advances further into Veggie Corp HQ, the account works towards the last a conflict with the magnetic head of Veggie Corp. This confounding figure, an image of the partnership's philosophy, turns into a definitive enemy. The account dives into the pioneer's inspirations, convictions, and the foundation of their faithfulness to vegetables. The magnetic pioneer arises as a mind boggling bad guy, and the confrontation turns into an emblematic battle, embodying the more extensive struggle between Veggie Corp and the powers of freedom.

The extraordinary peak of the Confrontation at Veggie Corp HQ unfurls as a crescendo of disclosures, penances, and the perfection of the characters' bends. The account cautiously explores the profound reverberation of key minutes — the victories, misfortunes, and the cost of rebellion. The charming pioneer, faced by the obstruction, turns into a powerful person whose development challenges assumptions of villainy. The standoff turns into a cauldron that produces the destiny of Veggie Corp HQ as well as the development of the characters who have embraced this challenging excursion.

In the repercussions of the standoff, the story enters an intelligent end result — a space to investigate the effect of the opposition's prosperity on the tragic world. Veggie Corp's control is broken, and the story catches the primary breaths of a general public freed from the harsh system. The individual accounts of the characters end up back at square one, offering conclusion to their singular bends while laying the foundation for the development of another request.

6.2 The team confronts Veggie Corp in an epic showdown.

In the climactic account of "Green Conflicts: The Veggie Feud," the group, manufactured through preliminaries, penetrations, and fights, remains on the cliff of an amazing standoff with Veggie Corp. This crucial part unfurls as a crescendo of strain, disclosures, and conflicts, where the characters defy the vegetable masters in a bid to break the harsh system. This investigation dives into the essential development prompting the amazing confrontation, the individual stakes of the characters, the tangled difficulties looked inside Veggie Corp's imposing fortress, and the groundbreaking peak that holds the destiny of the tragic world yet to be determined.

The essential development towards the legendary standoff is described by a tangible need to get a move on and expectation. Having uncovered the odious plans and genuine degree of Veggie Corp's control, the group turns into the key part of the opposition, energizing different groups, dispersing critical data, and planning for a definitive showdown. The account catches the aggregate breath held by the tragic culture, the force of defiance working as the obstruction blends around the group's administration.

As the group merges on Veggie Corp's fortress, the story distinctively paints the visual division between the chilly, forcing designs of the company and the mixed gathering not set in stone to challenge its matchless quality. The base camp, a post of mechanical may, turns into the setting for the looming conflict — a landmark where the powers of freedom try to destroy the actual center of Veggie Corp's power. The setting becomes emblematic, addressing the conflict between dictator control and the unwavering soul of obstruction.

The characters, presently fight solidified pioneers, wrestle with the individual stakes of the legendary standoff. The story dives into the close to home outcome of their excursion — the scars, misfortunes, and the unwavering assurance that pushes each person forward. Spurred by private quarrels, a journey for equity, or a craving to free society from vegetable masters, the heroes' singular inspirations interlace with the more extensive story, injecting the looming conflict with a rich embroidery of individual stories.

The arrangement to stand up to Veggie Corp turns into a story point of convergence, requiring perplexing planning, strategic splendor, and a solidarity of direction. The group, presently infiltrators as well as engineers of disobedience, explores the fragile dance of utilizing taboo information, taking advantage of Veggie Corp's weaknesses, and producing unions inside the obstruction. The story investigates the intricacies of administration, direction, and the heaviness of obligation as the group positions itself for the awe-inspiring confrontation.

Inside Veggie Corp's fortification, the difficulties become complex and misleading. The story unfurls a progression of hindrances — high level security frameworks, faithful masters, and the ruses of Veggie Corp's magnetic chief — that test the group's strength. The hallways of force inside the enterprise's base camp become a story maze, each step full of risk and the steady danger of revelation. The account ably catches the pressure, anticipation, and mental cost of exploring the core of Veggie Corp.

The implementers of Veggie Corp, expanded with vegetable-implanted innovations, arise as imposing foes. The story presents an increased condition of reconnaissance, persistent pursuit, and the consistently present gamble of openness. Each experience turns into a heartbeat beating second, a fragile dance on the slope of disclosure. The story underscores the stakes as the group moves through the hallways, undermining the full concentrations eyes of those faithful to the vegetable masters.

The mental cost of facing Veggie Corp turns into a story string, winding through the characters' encounters inside the fortification. The group wrestles with the steady danger of location, the heaviness of their main goal, and the information that the destiny of the obstruction relies on their prosperity. The inward struggles, neurosis, and snapshots of self-question become impactful account components, adding layers of intricacy to the characters and elevating the stakes of the incredible standoff.

Startling partners and disclosures inside Veggie Corp's fortress become account impetuses, infusing a component of unconventionality into the approaching conflict. The obstruction finds disagreeing voices inside the enterprise — people baffled by Veggie Corp's oppression and ready to help the defiance. These partners inside the central command become urgent account instruments, offering experiences, working with secretive developments, and making snapshots of pressure and interest inside the actual heart of the oppressor's area.

As the group advances further into Veggie Corp's fortification, the story works towards the last a conflict with the charming pioneer. This puzzling figure, the exemplification of Veggie Corp's philosophy, turns into a definitive enemy. The account dives into the pioneer's inspirations, convictions, and the base of their loyalty to vegetables. The magnetic pioneer arises as an intricate bad guy, and the incredible standoff turns into a representative battle, epitomizing the more extensive clash between Veggie Corp and the powers of freedom.

The extraordinary peak of the incredible confrontation unfurls as a crescendo of disclosures, penances, and the climax of the characters' bends. The story cautiously explores the close to home reverberation of key minutes — the victories, misfortunes, and the cost of resistance. The magnetic pioneer, faced by the group, turns into a powerful person whose development challenges assumptions of villainy. The incredible standoff turns into a cauldron that fashions the destiny of Veggie Corp as well as the development of the characters who have embraced this difficult excursion.

In the repercussions of the legendary confrontation, the story enters an intelligent outcome — a space to investigate the effect of the group's prosperity on the tragic world. Veggie Corp's control is broken, and the story catches the principal breaths of a general public freed from the severe system. The individual accounts of the characters end up back at square one, offering conclusion to their singular circular segments while laying the foundation for the rise of another request.

6.3 Highlight the intense battles, clever strategies, and unexpected twists.

In the embroidery of "Green Conflicts: The Veggie Quarrel," the legendary standoff between the opposition group and Veggie Corp unfurls with an ensemble of serious fights, sharp procedures, and surprising turns. This climactic section is a kaleidoscope of activity, tension, and key splendor as the characters explore the twisted difficulties inside Veggie Corp's impressive fortification. The story catches the beat beating snapshots of contention, the inventiveness of the group's strategies, and the unexpected turns that keep the two characters and perusers as eager and anxious as ever.

The extreme fights inside Veggie Corp's fortification become the point of convergence of the incredible confrontation. The story arranges scenes of instinctive battle, each conflict a demonstration of the versatility and abilities of the opposition group. As the group moves through the braced halls, they experience rushes of Veggie Corp masters increased with vegetable-implanted advances. The fights become serious, realistic successions — impacts of energy, gymnastic moves, and the conflict of weapons reverberating through the metallic bounds of the base camp.

The account paints distinctive pictures of the group going head to head against Veggie Corp's imposing powers, every part exhibiting their exceptional abilities and capacities. The pioneer, driven by an individual quarrel, arises as the vanguard, their assurance a revitalizing sob for the obstruction. The well informed virtuoso releases a deluge of developments, hacking into Veggie Corp's security frameworks and turning their own innovation against them. The secretive infiltrator explores the shadows, killing dangers with accuracy and artfulness. The big shot turns into a one-individual destroying team, crushing through Veggie Corp's protections with crude power.

In the midst of the serious fights, the story winds around snapshots of brotherhood and cooperation. The characters, limited by a mutual perspective, consistently coordinate their endeavors, every part depending on the qualities of the others. The close to home stakes uplift as the group defies Veggie Corp's authorities as well as the mental cost of the fights. The story dives into the characters' unseen conflicts, the heaviness of their central goal, and the penances made chasing after opportunity.

Cunning procedures arise as a story propensity, stringing through the incredible standoff. The group, equipped with prohibited information, takes advantage of Veggie Corp's weaknesses with vital splendor. The story explores the many-sided dance of trickery and deception as the obstruction utilizes diversionary strategies, confusion, and close quarters combat inside the base camp. The well informed virtuoso hacks into Veggie Corp's correspondence frameworks, taking care of deception and planting confusion among the masters.

Surprising turns become account impetuses, adding layers of intricacy to the awe-inspiring standoff. As the group advances through Veggie Corp's fortification, they uncover layers of misdirection and surprising coalitions. The account presents snapshots of interest and anticipation, where loyalties are tried, and characters face moral issues. Partners inside Veggie Corp's positions, baffled by the company's oppression, rise up out of the shadows, their inspirations and activities becoming vital in the unfurling account.

The magnetic head of Veggie Corp turns into an expert specialist, countering the opposition's moves with determined accuracy. The story investigates the pioneer's shrewdness, divulging a progression of traps, redirections, and mental fighting intended to break the soul of the opposition. The confrontation turns into a skirmish of brains, with the charming pioneer endeavoring to outsmart the group every step of the way. The unforeseen turns in the pioneer's methodology add a layer of flightiness, keeping the story strain tight.

The confounded difficulties inside Veggie Corp's fortification act as a story material for the serious fights and cunning techniques. The base camp, a mechanical wonder, turns into a person in itself — a foe that adjusts to the all opposition's moves. The story illustrates the passages loaded up with reconnaissance frameworks, robotized guards, and secret snares. The group explores through this high-stakes labyrinth, transforming each test into an open door to exhibit their creativity and flexibility.

As the legendary standoff arrives at its peak, the story works towards a groundbreaking peak. The serious fights, cunning procedures, and startling turns unite in a crescendo of disclosures, penances, and the summit of character circular segments. The magnetic pioneer, defied by the group, uncovers the genuine inspirations driving Veggie Corp's strength, adding a layer of profundity to the story. The account cautiously explores the close to home reverberation of key minutes — the victories, misfortunes, and the significant effect of the legendary standoff on both the characters and the tragic world.

In the result of the standoff, the story enters an intelligent conclusion — a space to investigate the outcomes of the group's prosperity. Veggie Corp's control is broken, and the story catches the primary breaths of a general public freed from the harsh system. The individual accounts of the characters end up back at square one, offering conclusion to their singular bends while laying the basis for the rise of another request.

7 |

Chapter 7

The Aftermath

Directly following the legendary standoff between the opposition group and Veggie Corp, the story unfurls into the significant outcome — a part that investigates the results, changes, and the reconfiguration of the tragic world in "Green Conflicts: The Veggie Grudge." This stage is set apart by the resonations of the obstruction's victory, the remaking of society freed from Veggie Corp's oppression, and the characters' route through the intricacies of a post-struggle scene.

The outcome starts with a scrutinizing resolution, as the residue chooses the milestone inside Veggie Corp's fortress. The story catches the quick fallout of the obstruction's triumph — the quiet that follows the disorder of fight, the reverberations of strides against the metallic halls, and the discernible feeling of freedom. The characters, when limited by the solitary reason for testing Veggie Corp, presently end up in a changed scene, wrestling with the ramifications of their prosperity.

The story winds through the prompt consequence, catching the close to home reverberation of the characters as they overview the vanquished region. The group, fight worn and genuinely scarred, considers the penances made, the misfortunes persevered, and the unstoppable soul that helped them through the legendary standoff. The consequence turns into a material for the characters' inner excursions, considering snapshots of contemplation, brotherhood, and the start of the mending system.

As the characters rise up out of Veggie Corp's fortress, the account extends to incorporate the more extensive results of the obstruction's triumph. The abused masses, motivated by the group's insubordination, ascend from the shadows and join the festival of recently discovered opportunity. The story investigates the celebration, help, and the deep breath of a general public freed from the shackles of vegetable masters. The outcome turns into a demonstration of the flexibility of the human soul and the persevering through journey for independence.

The cultural reproduction that follows the destruction of Veggie Corp turns into a story point of convergence. The story digs into the strategic difficulties of modifying, the reclamation of framework, and the foundation of another request. The characters, push into positions of authority by the exigencies of resistance, wrestle with the intricacies of administration, equity, and the fragile harmony among opportunity and request. The story explores the characters' development as pioneers, investigating their battles, wins, and the heaviness of obligation in molding a post-Veggie Corp society.

The result unfurls as an embroidery of individual person curves, each string meshing into the more extensive story of cultural remaking. The heroes, having risen up out of the cauldron of contention, face the test of coordinating once more into a world that has gone through a seismic shift. The account investigates their endeavors to accommodate the scars of fight, reclassify their characters, and explore the intricacies of newly discovered opportunity. Connections inside the group develop, as bonds produced in the cauldron of contention presently find new articulations in a world liberated from Veggie Corp's persecution.

At the same time, the charming head of Veggie Corp, vanquished in the legendary confrontation, turns into a story center. The result uncovers the outcomes of their loss — the destroying of Veggie Corp's framework, the openness of their dim mysteries, and the scattering of steadfast authorities. The story investigates the pioneer's inheritance, the waves of their impact, and the effect of their ruin on the remainders of Veggie Corp. The charming pioneer, when the epitome of Veggie Corp's belief system, presently turns into a wake up call reverberating through the repercussions.

Startling difficulties arise in the fallout, testing the strength of the recently freed society. The account presents the intricacies of force vacuums, factional questions, and the remainders of Veggie Corp's impact endeavoring to refocus. The characters, having conquered the outer danger of Veggie Corp, should now explore the conflicts under the surface of a general public in transition. The outcome turns into a story investigation of the fragile harmony among freedom and the possible entanglements of a world without the overall control of vegetable masters.

The story illustrates the cultural change, catching the visual differences between the tragic past and the early future. The once sterile designs of Veggie Corp's fortification currently stand as landmarks to opposition, embellished with images of opportunity and versatility. The story investigates the recovering of spaces, the reusing of innovation, and the reintegration of nature into a world that had been overwhelmed by vegetables. The repercussions turns into a visual illustration for the victory of humankind over counterfeit control.

Individual retributions become vital to the outcome account, as characters face the results of their activities and choices during the legendary standoff. The account digs into the characters' ethical problems, the shades of dim that arise chasing freedom, and the eerie ghosts of the past. The outcome turns into a space for recovery, pardoning, and the characters' wrestling with the shades of profound quality in a world rising up out of the shadows of Veggie Corp's control.

The outcome story unfurls in a nonlinear style, entwining snapshots of reflection, cultural reproduction, and individual retributions. The characters' accounts, presently interconnected with the more extensive cultural embroidery, become a mosaic of strength, change, and the getting through reverberations of the legendary confrontation. The story catches the subtleties of a world experiencing significant change, where the scars of contention coincide with the expanding any desire for a fresh start.

As the story works towards its decision, the result turns into a material for the characters' last changes. The group, when different people limited by a shared adversary, presently remains as draftsmen of a freed society. The story investigates the characters' heritages, the effect of their excursion on the tragic world, and the getting through examples of the legendary standoff. The determination turns into a snapshot of reflection, festivity, and the affirmation that the outcome isn't simply a closure yet a preamble to another part in the tale of Green Conflicts.

The result in "Green Conflicts: The Veggie Feud" is a story material that investigates the outcomes, changes, and cultural reconfigurations following the legendary confrontation. Through contemplative minutes, cultural remaking, and individual retributions, the fallout turns into a nuanced investigation of freedom and the intricacies that emerge in the outcome of contention. As the characters and society rise up out of the shadows of Veggie Corp's oppression, the fallout turns into a demonstration of the unstoppable soul of mankind and the persevering through mission for a superior world.

7.1 Consequences and Fallout

As the residue gets comfortable the outcome of the incredible standoff between the opposition group and Veggie Corp, the account digs into the significant results and aftermath that resound all through the tragic universe of "Green Conflicts: The Veggie Grudge.

" This period of the story investigates the multifaceted trap of repercussions originating from the ruin of Veggie Corp, tending to the quick fallout, cultural movements, individual changes, and the unfamiliar domains that anticipate the two characters and the freed society.

The prompt consequence is set apart by an insightful quiet that drops upon the milestone inside Veggie Corp's fortification. The story catches the strange peacefulness that follows the racket of contention, underscoring the ghostliness of a space once overwhelmed by the harsh control of vegetable masters. The characters, actually staggering from the force of the awe-inspiring confrontation, explore through the left-overs of Veggie Corp's stronghold. The outcome turns into a story space for reflection, as the group wrestles with the profound and actual cost of their successful insubordination.

The results of the opposition's victory stretch out past the quick consequence, pervading the more extensive cultural scene. The story unfurls as a mosaic of interconnected stories, each mirroring the reper-cussions of Veggie Corp's defeat on different features of the tragic world. The persecuted masses, enlivened by the group's resistance, ascend from the shadows and take part in the aggregate celebration. The story inves-tigates the cultural therapy, the shedding of the aggregate injury caused by Veggie Corp, and the development of a freshly discovered trust that waves through the freed society.

The recreation of the tragic world turns into a focal concentration as the results unfurl. The story explores the calculated difficulties of revamping — fixing foundation, restoring correspondence organiza-tions, and reestablishing fundamental administrations. The characters, presently push into influential positions, wrestle with the intricacies of administration, manufacturing a way toward another request that looks to stay away from the entanglements of Veggie Corp's severe system. The reproduction turns into a story material for investigating topics of strength, versatility, and the fragile harmony among opportunity and design.

Cultural movements become apparent as the outcomes of Veggie Corp's ruin keep on unfurling. The story catches the advancing ele-ments among the freed masses, investigating the freshly discovered feeling of organization and self-assurance. Groups that once existed in the shadows start to state their personalities, adding to the forming of a post-Veggie Corp society. The results become a story investigation of the fragile balance between aggregate freedom and the likely cracks inside a general public exploring unknown regions.

Individual changes are woven into the texture of results, as characters wrestle with the outcome of the incredible confrontation. The account digs into the mental effect of the characters' excursion — the scars, injuries, and the developing comprehension of their jobs in the tragic world. Connections inside the group go through additional transformation as the characters explore the intricacies of newly discovered opportunity, manufacturing further associations in light of shared encounters and the common weight of their defiant victory.

The magnetic head of Veggie Corp, however vanquished in the legendary confrontation, keeps on creating a long shaded area in the consequence. The results of their loss unwind the layers of Veggie Corp's impact — the destroying of its framework, the openness of dull insider facts, and the scattering of faithful authorities. The story investigates the leftovers of Veggie Corp endeavoring to refocus, adding a component of waiting danger and eccentricism to the results. The charming pioneer's inheritance turns into an unpleasant phantom, moving the freed society to face the reverberations of its severe past.

Surprising difficulties arise in the fallout, testing the versatility of the recently freed society. The story presents the intricacies of force vacuums, factional questions, and leftovers of Veggie Corp's impact endeavoring to take advantage of the weaknesses inside the freed society. The characters, having conquered the outside danger of Veggie Corp, presently go up against conflicts under the surface as they explore the strange domains of post-struggle administration. The outcomes become a story investigation of the fragile harmony among freedom and the likely entanglements inside a world liberated from the general control of vegetable masters.

The results and aftermath are not absent any trace of moral uncertainty, as characters face the moral ramifications of their activities during the incredible confrontation. The account digs into the characters' ethical retributions, the shades of dim that arise chasing freedom, and the eerie apparitions of the past that wait in the fallout. Subjects of recovery, pardoning, and the characters' wrestling with the intricacies of ethical quality become essential to the outcomes story, adding layers of profundity and reflection.

The cultural change is imagined through the account focal point, catching the distinct differentiations between the tragic past and the incipient future. The once sterile designs of Veggie Corp's fortification presently stand as landmarks to obstruction, embellished with images of opportunity and versatility. The story investigates the recovering of spaces, the reusing of innovation, and the reintegration of nature into a world that had been overwhelmed by vegetables. The results story turns into a visual representation for the victory of mankind over counterfeit control.

Individual retributions become a fundamental story string inside the outcomes and aftermath. Characters face the outcomes of their activities and choices during the incredible confrontation, wrestling with the ethical intricacies of their insubordination. The story dives into the characters' conflicts under the surface, the heaviness of their decisions, and the mission for individual reclamation in the fallout. The results become a space for characters to face the shades of profound quality in a world rising up out of the shadows of Veggie Corp's control.

As the story works towards its decision, the outcomes and aftermath become a material for the characters' last changes. The group, when unique people limited by a shared adversary, presently remains as draftsmen of a freed society. The story investigates the characters' heritages, the effect of their excursion on the tragic world, and the persevering through illustrations of the awe-inspiring confrontation. The determination turns into a snapshot of reflection, festivity, and the affirmation that the results and aftermath are a closure as well as a preface to another part in the tale of Green Conflicts.

7.2 Explore the aftermath of the battle and the impact on the world.

As the reverberations of the legendary standoff between the opposition group and Veggie Corp resound, the account unfurls into the many-sided result of the fight, investigating the significant effect on the tragic world in "Green Conflicts: The Veggie Feud." This period of the story dives into the expansive outcomes, cultural changes, individual reflections, and the unknown regions that entice characters and the freed society.

The quick repercussions paints a scene of the vanquished milestone inside Veggie Corp's fortification. The story catches the frightful quiet that dives after the tempest of contention, underlining the unpleasant tranquility of a space once overwhelmed by the harsh control of vegetable masters. The characters, actually washed in the adrenaline of triumph and the lingering strain of fight, explore through the leftovers of Veggie Corp's fort. The consequence turns into a pondering material, a story space for reflection as the group wrestles with the close to home and actual cost of their fruitful disobedience.

The outcomes of the obstruction's victory echo through the tragic world, making a permanent imprint on the cultural scene. The story unfurls as an interconnected embroidery of stories, each string meshing into the more extensive account of change. The abused masses, propelled by the group's resistance, ascend from the shadows, partaking in the aggregate celebration that moves throughout the freed society. The story dives into the cultural therapy, the shedding of aggregate injury incurred by Veggie Corp, and the development of a freshly discovered trust that saturates each side of the tragic world.

Cultural change turns into a focal subject as the outcomes of Veggie Corp's defeat keep on unfurling. The story explores the calculated difficulties of modifying — a careful interaction including the maintenance of foundation, the restoration of correspondence organizations, and the reclamation of fundamental administrations. The characters, push into influential positions, wrestle with the intricacies of administration, producing a way toward another request that looks to keep away from the traps of Veggie Corp's severe system. The reproduction turns into a story investigation of flexibility, versatility, and the fragile harmony among opportunity and design.

The repercussions is described by moving elements among the freed masses, denoting the development of cultural connections. The account catches the freshly discovered feeling of organization and self-assurance that saturates the general population. Groups that once worked in the shadows start to declare their characters, adding to the forming of a post-Veggie Corp society. The outcomes story turns into a reflection on the fragile harmony between aggregate freedom and the expected cracks inside a general public exploring unknown regions.

Individual changes are entwined into the texture of the outcome, as characters wrestle with the results of the amazing standoff. The story digs into the mental effect of the characters' excursion — the scars, injuries, and the developing comprehension of their jobs in the tragic world. Connections inside the group go through additional transformation as characters explore the intricacies of freshly discovered opportunity, producing further associations in view of shared encounters and the common weight of their victorious disobedience.

The charming head of Veggie Corp, however vanquished, keeps on creating a shaded area in the result, adding layers of intricacy to the story. The results of their loss disentangle Veggie Corp's impact — the destroying of its framework, the openness of dull insider facts, and the scattering of steadfast implementers. The story investigates the leftovers of Veggie Corp endeavoring to refocus, presenting a component of waiting danger and flightiness to the result. The charming pioneer's inheritance turns into an eerie phantom, moving the freed society to defy the reverberations of its harsh past.

Unforeseen difficulties arise, testing the versatility of the recently freed society and adding subtlety to the results account. The story presents the intricacies of force vacuums, factional debates, and leftovers of Veggie Corp's impact endeavoring to take advantage of weaknesses inside the freed society. The characters, having defeated the outer danger of Veggie Corp, presently face unseen conflicts as they explore the unfamiliar domains of post-struggle administration. The outcomes story turns into a nuanced investigation of the sensitive harmony among freedom and the expected traps inside a world liberated from the overall control of vegetable masters.

The cultural change is envisioned through the story focal point, catching the distinct differentiations between the tragic past and the incipient future. The once sterile designs of Veggie Corp's fortress presently stand as landmarks to opposition, enhanced with images of opportunity and flexibility. The story investigates the recovering of spaces, the reusing of innovation, and the reintegration of nature into a world that had been overwhelmed by vegetables. The outcomes story turns into a visual similitude for the victory of humankind over fake control.

Individual retributions become a fundamental account string inside the outcome, as characters defy the results of their activities during the awe-inspiring confrontation. The story dives into the characters' conflicts under the surface, the heaviness of their decisions, and the journey for individual reclamation in the result. Subjects of ethical quality, recovery, and absolution become basic to the outcomes story, adding layers of profundity and contemplation.

As the story works toward its decision, the result turns into a material for the characters' last changes. The group, when dissimilar people limited by a shared adversary, presently remains as planners of a freed society. The story investigates the characters' heritages, the effect of their excursion on the tragic world, and the getting through examples of the awe-inspiring confrontation. The decision turns into a snapshot of reflection, festivity, and the affirmation that the repercussions isn't simply a completion however a preamble to another part in the narrative of Green Conflicts.

7.3 Address the changes in society and the characters' personal growth.

As the residue settles from the climactic fight between the opposition group and Veggie Corp, the story unfurls into a strong investigation of the progressions in the public eye and the significant self-awareness experienced by the characters in "Green Conflicts: The Veggie Feud." This period of the story dives into the complexities of cultural development, looking at the subtleties of a world freed from vegetable masters, and entwining it with the rich embroidery of individual person bends.

The cultural changes exude as a substantial propensity in the fallout of Veggie Corp's loss. The story explores the scene of a changed society, freed from the harsh control of vegetable masters. The once-muffled voices of the persecuted masses ascend in celebration, making an orchestra of aggregate opportunity. The story digs into the visual change of metropolitan spaces — when clean under Veggie Corp's impact — presently enhanced with dynamic images of opposition and versatility. The progressions in the public eye become a demonstration of the unstoppable soul of humankind, denoting the development of another request that tries to move away from the shackles of the past.

Primary changes in administration and framework become significant components in the cultural advancement story. The characters, push into influential positions by the exigencies of insubordination, wrestle with the intricacies of reconstructing.

The account investigates the foundation of new correspondence organizations, the maintenance of fundamental administrations, and the fragile harmony among opportunity and the requirement for organized administration. The cultural changes story turns into a reflection on the versatile limit of the freed masses, as they explore the unfamiliar regions of post-Veggie Corp remaking.

The investigation of cultural movements interlaces with the self-awareness of the characters, making a story orchestra that reverberates with close to home profundity. The heroes, having risen up out of the pot of contention, go through significant changes that reflect the progressions in the more extensive society they freed. The account dives into the characters' inner excursions, investigating the scars, wins, and developing comprehension of their parts in the tragic world.

Connections inside the opposition group advance as characters explore the intricacies of freshly discovered opportunity. The fellowship, produced in the cauldron of contention, changes into more profound associations in light of shared encounters and the aggregate weight of their victorious defiance. The account winds around snapshots of weakness, strength, and the implicit bonds that integrate the characters. As they go up against the progressions in the public eye, the characters additionally face the progressions inside themselves and one another, further enhancing the woven artwork of self-awareness.

The magnetic head of Veggie Corp, however vanquished, keeps on creating a shaded area in the fallout, molding the characters' self-awareness story. The disclosures about Veggie Corp's dull mysteries and the genuine inspirations driving the vegetable masters force the characters to defy moral problems and moral ambiguities. The magnetic pioneer turns into an unearthly presence, a sign of the scarce difference among freedom and the potential entanglements that wait inside the human mind. The characters wrestle with the self-awareness story, scrutinizing the shades of ethical quality and the waiting effect of Veggie Corp's impact on their own personalities.

Unforeseen difficulties arise as a story impetus, testing the strength of the recently freed society and becoming cauldrons for individual person development. The remainders of Veggie Corp endeavor to refocus, taking advantage of the weaknesses inside the freed society. The characters, having defeated the outer danger of Veggie Corp, presently face subtle conflicts — factional debates, power vacuums, and the intricacies of exploring a world untethered from the general control of vegetable masters. The story ably interlaces the cultural changes with the characters' self-awareness, stressing the advantageous connection between the two.

The self-awareness story turns into a space for recovery, pardoning, and the characters' wrestling with the intricacies of profound quality in a world rising up out of the shadows of Veggie Corp's control.

The unseen conflicts and moral difficulties looked by the characters add to their development, molding their ways of life as designers of a freed society. The account investigates the nuanced layers of self-awareness, depicting the characters not as static legends but rather as unique people molded by the cauldron of contention and the progressions in the tragic world they changed.

As the characters and society explore the unfamiliar domains of post-Veggie Corp freedom, the story works toward an intelligent outcome. The self-improvement circular segments arrive at their pinnacle as the characters find a sense of peace with the results of their activities, the penances made, and the getting through effect of their insubordination. The cultural changes story tracks down goal in the characters' developing jobs as pioneers and planners of another request. The outcome turns into a space for festivity, reflection, and the affirmation that self-awareness and cultural development are not direct however recurrent cycles.

The investigation of changes in the public eye and the characters' self-improvement in "Green Conflicts: The Veggie Quarrel" frames a story embroidery that rises above the limits of a tragic struggle. From the perspective of cultural development, primary changes, and self-improvement, the story turns into an immortal investigation of human versatility, flexibility, and the getting through mission for a superior world. The characters, having confronted the pot of contention and arisen as draftsmen of a freed society, stand as demonstrations of the unyielding soul of humankind even with severe control.

Chapter 8

Epilogue

The epilog of "Green Conflicts: The Veggie Grudge" unfurls as a thoughtful reflection, a story space where the reverberations of the legendary standoff resound through the changed tragic world. This closing part winds around together the waiting results, cultural advancement, individual person circular segments, and the getting through examples of the defiance to Veggie Corp.

As the story subsides into the epilog, the repercussions of the opposition group's victory endure, creating a long shaded area over the freed society. The result of Veggie Corp's loss keeps on forming the tragic scene, with remainders of the vegetable masters endeavoring to refocus and recover control. The story investigates the sensitive harmony between the freshly discovered opportunity and the expected resurgence of harsh powers, making a nuanced scenery for the epilog.

Cultural development turns into a point of convergence as the epilog digs into the complexities of a world untethered from Veggie Corp's impact. The story explores the primary changes in administration, the reconstruction of cultural standards, and the fragile dance between individual independence and aggregate request. The freed masses, once mistreated, presently stand as designers of their fate, by and large exploring the unknown regions of a post-Veggie Corp time. The epilog turns into a material for investigating the versatility and flexibility innate in the human soul.

Primary changes in the tragic world manifest outwardly, delineating the groundbreaking force of disobedience. Metropolitan spaces once overwhelmed by the sterile impact of Veggie Corp's control currently bear the characteristics of obstruction and flexibility. Landmarks to the insubordination ascend in the midst of the cityscape, decorated with images that recognize the battle for opportunity. The account investigates the reusing of Veggie Corp's foundation, transforming once-abusive designs into signals of opposition and tokens of the victory of humankind over fake control.

The characters, having explored the pot of contention and arisen as impetuses of cultural change, go through a significant development in the epilog. The story digs into the self-improvement bends, investigating how the characters accommodate with the outcomes of their activities, the penances made, and the ethical intricacies looked during the defiance. Every hero wrestles with the shadows of their past, fashioning a way toward reclamation, pardoning, and a more profound comprehension of their jobs in the reshaped tragic world.

The connections inside the obstruction group keep on advancing in the epilog, mirroring the persevering through bonds manufactured in the cauldron of contention. The fellowship, tried by the power of the disobedience, changes into a strong groundwork whereupon the characters construct their fates. The account investigates the interchange of connections — kinships that develop, coalitions that persevere, and the implicit comprehension that ties the characters together. The epilog turns into a space for the characters to explore the intricacies of their associations in a world reshaped by their aggregate resistance.

The charming head of Veggie Corp, however crushed, stays a phantom presence in the epilog — a waiting sign of the more obscure shades of force and control. The story uncovers the remainders of Veggie Corp endeavoring to refocus, presenting a component of vulnerability and strain. The epilog turns into a story investigation of the consistently present danger, underlining the requirement for watchfulness solidarity in a general public actually recuperating from the injuries caused by the vegetable masters.

Surprising difficulties arise, testing the flexibility of the freed society and the actual characters. The story presents the intricacies of force vacuums, inner debates, and leftovers of Veggie Corp's impact endeavoring to take advantage of weaknesses. The characters, having beaten the outside danger of Veggie Corp, end up exploring the complexities of administration, ethical quality, and the sensitive balance between individual opportunity and cultural union. The epilog turns into a space for investigating the continuous battles innate in building a supportable future in the repercussions of defiance.

The self-awareness story is joined with the more extensive cultural changes, making a consistent embroidery that catches the substance of the epilog. The characters, presently representative figures in the reshaped tragic world, stand at the junction of individual fates and aggregate liability. The account investigates the recurrent idea of self-awareness, underscoring that the excursion toward self-disclosure is a continuous cycle, intelligent of the always changing scene they helped fashion.

As the characters and society explore the intricacies of the post-Veggie Corp time, the story works toward an intelligent outcome in the epilog. The heroes, having confronted the pot of contention and arisen as modelers of a freed society, stand at the edge of another part in their lives. The end result turns into a snapshot of reflection, a space for praising the victories, recognizing the misfortunes, and pondering the persevering through examples of the insubordination. The epilog turns into a material for pondering the unstoppable soul of humankind even with mistreatment.

In the closing snapshots of the epilog, the story investigates the tradition of the obstruction against Veggie Corp. Landmarks to the insubordination stand as demonstrations of the flexibility and fortitude of the people who challenged the vegetable masters. The story catches the murmurs of history, guaranteeing that the examples learned and the penances made are not neglected. The epilog turns into a story vessel for the transmission of aggregate memory, underscoring the significance of recalling the past as society outlines its course into a questionable however freed future.

The epilog of "Green Conflicts: The Veggie Feud" fills in as a thoughtful reflection on the result of the defiance, the getting through outcomes, and the groundbreaking force of individual and aggregate flexibility. Through the investigation of cultural changes, self-improvement, and the repeating idea of self-disclosure, the epilog turns into an immortal investigation of the human soul's ability to beat persecution and shape a superior world. The characters, having risen up out of the pot of contention, stand as encouraging signs in a tragic world everlastingly changed by their rebellion against the vegetable masters.

8.1 Seeds of Change

"Seeds of Progress" unfurls as an enrapturing section inside the story of "Green Conflicts: The Veggie Quarrel," investigating the groundbreaking force of thoughts, developments, and the unyielding human soul in reshaping a tragic world. This section digs into the beginnings of a resistance that develops from the fruitful soil of discontent, at last growing into an impressive power against the harsh system of Veggie Corp.

The seeds of progress are planted in the ripe ground of cultural discontent, where the account follows the foundations of opposition against the consistently developing impact of Veggie Corp. The tragic world, at first quelled by the apparently kindhearted control of vegetable masters, hides pockets of difference and discontent among the mistreated masses. The story reveals the inconspicuous mumbles of obstruction, the murmurs of the individuals who harbor a well established longing for independence, and the seeds of progress that will later prosper into an undeniable insubordination.

The story strips back the layers of Veggie Corp's publicity machine, uncovering the breaks in the exterior of kindness. As the abused masses become progressively mindful of the hazier real factors hiding underneath the surface, the seeds of progress track down prolific ground in the bafflement and aggregate craving for opportunity. The story catches the unfolding acknowledgment that the vegetables, when seen as big-hearted suppliers, are, as a matter of fact, guileful puppeteers controlling the strings of society for their own benefit.

Individual demonstrations of disobedience arise as antecedents to the bigger resistance, featuring the flexibility and fortitude of the people who try to challenge Veggie Corp's control. The account presents characters who, driven by an inborn feeling of equity, become accidental grower of the seeds of progress. Their little demonstrations of disobedience, whether through rebellious correspondences or secret social occasions, lay the foundation for a more critical uprising. The story meshes these singular stories into an embroidery of obstruction, representing the different inspirations that fuel the seeds of progress.

The charming head of Veggie Corp, however at first careless in regards to the expanding dispute, detects the propensities of disobedience. The account investigates their endeavors to subdue the seeds of progress through expanded reconnaissance, promulgation, and the control of public insight. Be that as it may, the more Veggie Corp fixes its grasp, the more the seeds of progress track down safe-haven in the hearts of those longing for independence. The story winds around an unobtrusive dance among oppressor and the mistreated, as the seeds of progress discreetly sprout underneath the full concentrations eyes of Veggie Corp.

The story presents vital minutes that act as impetuses for the seeds of progress to grow and flourish. These snapshots of disclosure, whether through openness to Veggie Corp's dull privileged insights or individual misfortunes incurred by the vegetable masters, electrify the abused masses. The story catches the tangible change in shared awareness, as the seeds of progress advance from unobtrusive mumbles to reverberating statements of resistance. The story works towards a crescendo, where the persecuted masses, powered by the seeds of progress, start to scrutinize the laid out request and imagine a world liberated from the grasp of Veggie Corp.

The development of charming pioneers inside the prospering defiance turns into a story point of convergence. The seeds of progress track down champions — people whose moxy, vital intuition, and capacity to verbalize the aggregate complaints move the disobedience into a considerable power. The story investigates the enrollment of different voices into the overlap of the opposition, exhibiting the mosaic of abilities, foundations, and inspirations that merge under the standard of progress. The charming pioneers become courses for the seeds of progress, directing the aggregate will of individuals into a bound together front against Veggie Corp.

The story unfurls the beginning phases of the insubordination — the surreptitious gatherings, incendiary correspondences, and demonstrations of rebellion that mark the uprising's nascent stage. The seeds of progress, presently grew into a grassroots development, rock the boat and make swells inside the tragic world. The story explores the intricacies of clandestine tasks, coalitions fashioned in the shadows, and the fragile dance between the revolutionary chiefs and Veggie Corp's implementers. The story catches the pressure and vulnerability that penetrates the defiance's beginning phases, as the seeds of progress bloom into an imposing power against the vegetable masters.

As the insubordination picks up speed, the account investigates the strategic and vital difficulties looked by the magnetic pioneers and their adherents. The seeds of progress, when established in the hearts of the mistreated, presently manifest in composed activities pointed toward destroying Veggie Corp's control. The story dives into the complexities of close quarters combat, disruption of Veggie Corp's framework, and the mobilizing cries that reverberation through the tragic world. The story winds around snapshots of win and mishaps, stressing the versatility of the seeds of progress notwithstanding misfortune.

The magnetic pioneers become story key parts, exemplifying the groundbreaking force of the seeds of progress. The story investigates their own battles, penances, and the heaviness of administration as they guide the defiance toward its crescendo. The pioneers' singular development becomes interwoven with the account of the seeds of progress, accentuating that the insurgency isn't just about cultural change yet in addition the advancement of the people who champion the reason.

The account arrives at its apex as the disobedience finishes in an amazing standoff against Veggie Corp. The seeds of progress, having developed into an imposing power, conflict with the settled in powers in a last a showdown that will decide the destiny of the tragic world. The account catches the force of the fight, the reverberations of insubordination resonating through the freed masses, and the emblematic load of the seeds of progress happening as expected. The peak turns into a demonstration of the steadfast soul of the people who considered testing the severe system and the extraordinary power intrinsic in the seeds of progress.

As the residue settles from the amazing confrontation, the account advances into the outcome — the results, cultural movements, individual changes, and the strange domains that anticipate. The seeds of progress, having satisfied their progressive reason, presently make a permanent imprint on the tragic world. The story winds around a nuanced investigation of the outcome, catching the intricacy of cultural development, individual development, and the getting through tradition of the insubordination energized by the seeds of progress.

"Seeds of Progress" inside "Green Conflicts: The Veggie Grudge" fills in as a convincing part that disentangles the groundbreaking force of disobedience, thoughts, and the unyielding human soul. Through the investigation of cultural discontent, individual demonstrations of rebellion, the development of charming pioneers, and the inevitable uprising against Veggie Corp, the story lays out a striking representation of the seeds of progress growing from the rich ground of persecution. This part turns into an immortal investigation of the human ability to challenge the laid out request, plant the seeds of change, and support the blazes of disobedience that shine brilliantly against the shadows of oppression.

8.2 Conclude the story with a glimpse into the new world order.

The closing section of "Green Conflicts: The Veggie Quarrel" rises above the wild struggle, diving into the outcome of the resistance and offering an all encompassing perspective on the new world request that rises out of the cinders of Veggie Corp's severe rule. As the story winds around its last strings, it turns into a material for investigating the cultural movements, individual changes, and the strange regions that entice following the legendary standoff.

The fallout spreads out as a scene of cultural change, delineating the permanent effect of the insubordination on the tragic world. The once-sterile designs that bore Veggie Corp's engraving presently stand as landmarks to obstruction, embellished with images of opportunity and flexibility. The story explores the strategic difficulties of remaking — a fastidious cycle including the maintenance of foundation, the restoration of correspondence organizations, and the rebuilding of fundamental administrations. The freed society, presently confronted with the errand of revamping, turns into a pot for strength, flexibility, and the sensitive balance among opportunity and design.

Cultural development becomes the dominant focal point as the story investigates the rise of another world request. The characters, push into influential positions, wrestle with the intricacies of administration, manufacturing a way toward a general public that tries to keep away from the traps of Veggie Corp's severe system. The account catches the fragile dance between individual independence and aggregate request, underlining the nuanced talks that shape the underpinnings of the freed world. The new world request story turns into a reflection on the conceivable outcomes and difficulties innate in making a general public liberated from the overall control of vegetable masters.

Primary changes manifest outwardly, displaying the groundbreaking force of defiance. Metropolitan spaces, when overwhelmed by the sterile impact of Veggie Corp, presently bear the characteristics of obstruction and versatility. Landmarks to the insubordination ascend in the midst of the cityscape, enhanced with dynamic images that honor the battle for opportunity. The story investigates the recovering of spaces, the reusing of innovation, and the reintegration of nature into a world that had been overwhelmed by vegetables. The new world request story turns into a visual illustration for the victory of mankind over fake control.

The characters, having explored the cauldron of contention, go through significant individual changes in the consequence. The account digs into their interior processes — the scars, wins, and developing comprehension of their parts in the reshaped tragic world. Connections inside the obstruction group keep on advancing as characters explore the intricacies of freshly discovered opportunity. The brotherhood, tried by the power of the resistance, changes into more profound associations in view of shared encounters and the aggregate weight of their victorious stand. The account investigates the complexities of connections — kinships that extend, collusions that persevere, and the implicit comprehension that ties the characters together.

The charming head of Veggie Corp, however crushed, keeps on creating a shaded area in the fallout, adding layers of intricacy to the story. The results of their loss unwind Veggie Corp's impact — the destroying of its framework, the openness of dull insider facts, and the scattering of faithful implementers. The story investigates the remainders of Veggie Corp endeavoring to refocus, presenting a component of waiting danger and eccentricism to the consequence. The charming pioneer's heritage turns into an eerie phantom, moving the freed society to defy the reverberations of its harsh past.

Surprising difficulties arise, testing the strength of the recently freed society and adding subtlety to the result story. The story presents the intricacies of force vacuums, factional questions, and remainders of Veggie Corp's impact endeavoring to take advantage of weaknesses inside the freed society. The characters, having beaten the outside danger of Veggie Corp, presently face subtle conflicts as they explore the unfamiliar regions of post-struggle administration. The outcome story turns into a nuanced investigation of the fragile harmony among freedom and the expected entanglements inside a world liberated from the overall control of vegetable masters.

As the story works toward its determination, the repercussions turns into a material for the characters' last changes. The group, when divergent people limited by a shared adversary, presently remains as draftsmen of a freed society. The account investigates the characters' heritages, the effect of their excursion on the tragic world, and the getting through illustrations of the amazing confrontation. The decision turns into a snapshot of reflection, festivity, and the affirmation that the consequence isn't simply a consummation however a preamble to another part in the narrative of Green Conflicts.

The investigation of the consequence in "Green Conflicts: The Veggie Quarrel" shapes a story embroidery that rises above the limits of a tragic struggle. Through the prompt repercussions, cultural movements, individual changes, and the strange regions that anticipate, the story turns into an immortal investigation of human versatility, cultural development, and the getting through journey for a superior world. The characters, having confronted the pot of contention and arisen as planners of a freed society, stand as demonstrations of the dauntless soul of humankind even with harsh control. The new world request that arises isn't simply an impression of cultural change yet a demonstration of the seeds of progress and the getting through tradition of disobedience.

8.3 Leave room for the possibility of future adventures or developments in the world of vegetables and rebellion.

As the story of "Green Conflicts: The Veggie Feud" finishes up, it abandons the waiting reverberations of the incredible clash and the beginning of another period. However, inside this goal, the account purposely leaves space for the enticing chance of future undertakings and advancements in the realm of vegetables and disobedience. The determination turns into an entry, to conclusion, however to the possibility of unknown domains and untold stories ready to be revealed.

The fallout unfurls as a unique scene, with the freed society exploring the unknown domains of post-Veggie Corp administration. The story investigates the fragile harmony among opportunity and request, exhibiting the advancing designs of the new world request. While the quick dangers of Veggie Corp have been vanquished, the story alludes to the intricacies and difficulties intrinsic in keeping a freed society. Power vacuums, factional questions, and remainders of Veggie Corp's impact become account strings that mesh into the texture of the result, leaving openings for future experiences and improvements.

Cultural advancement stays a continuous account investigation, and the end deliberately leaves specific perspectives unassuming. The freed masses, having ascended from the shadows, keep on forming the shapes of their general public. The account alludes to the rise of new philosophies, developments, and voices inside the freed world. As the characters wrestle with the obligations of administration, the potential for unique ways and unanticipated improvements turns into a rich ground for future stories. The decision turns into a sign of approval for the smoothness of cultural development, passing on space for perusers to envision the heap headings the freed world could take.

Primary changes in the tragic world are portrayed outwardly, accentuating the extraordinary force of defiance. Notwithstanding, the account purposefully leaves specific components in motion. The landmarks to obstruction, when images of disobedience, stand as fresh starts anticipating the accounts that will decorate them. The reused innovation, presently quiet observer to the disobedience's victory, holds the potential for revelations and developments yet to be disclosed. The account leaves these obvious signs as breadcrumbs, welcoming perusers to envision the untold stories that might rise up out of the freed scenes.

The characters, playing played vital parts in the resistance, end up at the junction of their own excursions. The end indicates the chance of new difficulties, unanticipated coalitions, and neglected features of the characters' personalities. While the quick curve of their story might be settled, the account purposefully passes on holes that welcome perusers to guess on the characters' prospects. The individual changes saw in the consequence become seeds for possible future stories, offering a material for the characters to develop and set out on new undertakings.

The charming head of Veggie Corp, however crushed, waits as a ghostly presence in the result. The story proposes that the leftovers of Veggie Corp, endeavoring to refocus, may present future difficulties to the freed society. The dim mysteries and secret plans alluded to in the end become story snares, leaving space for the resurgence of a danger that could push the characters into new contentions and quandaries. The crushed pioneer's heritage turns into a story conundrum, portending the potential for waiting shadows and neglected profundities.

Surprising difficulties arise, displaying the flexibility of the freed society and the characters. The story presents the intricacies of inside debates and fights for control inside the post-resistance scene. The seeds of potential struggles are planted inside the freed society, giving story strings that might disentangle in later stories. The end intentionally leaves these difficulties unsettled, making spaces for future experiences that might investigate the complexities of administration, ethical quality, and the fragile harmony between individual opportunity and cultural attachment.

As the story works toward its decision, the characters end up remaining on the cliff of another part. The freed world turns into a material for possible joint efforts, partnerships, and clashes that might characterize the characters' prospects. The account intentionally avoids taking care of every single potential issue, leaving specific inquiries unanswered and certain fates unwritten. The determination turns into a platform for future undertakings, with the characters ready to investigate strange regions and face difficulties yet concealed.

In the finishing up snapshots of the story, a feeling of expectation and vulnerability waits in the freed air. The goal turns into a preface, welcoming perusers to really ponder the horde prospects that might unfurl in the realm of vegetables and resistance. The story purposely leaves holes in the woven artwork, passing on space for perusers to imagine future accounts, untold stories, and unanticipated turns of events. The end turns into a greeting for perusers to become co-makers of the world, effectively partaking in the speculative excursion past the bounds of the last pages.

The purposeful transparency of the end in "Green Conflicts: The Veggie Grudge" establishes the groundwork for the chance of future experiences and advancements in the realm of vegetables and disobedience. The freed society, characters, and the leftovers of Veggie Corp become account seeds holding back to grow into new stories. The decision turns into a demonstration of the story's dynamic nature, welcoming perusers to draw in their creative mind, investigate unfamiliar domains, and imagine the vast potential outcomes that lie into the great beyond.

9

Chapter 9

Rebuilding Society

The outcome of the legendary struggle in "Green Conflicts: The Veggie Quarrel" introduces a significant period of cultural change and reproduction. The account moves its concentration toward the many-sided course of modifying society, catching the difficulties, wins, and strange regions that unfurl directly following Veggie Corp's loss. As the residue settles and the freed masses stand in the midst of the leftovers of the old request, the story turns into a material for the flexibility of mankind, the intricacies of administration, and the fragile harmony among opportunity and design.

The remaking of society turns into a story point of convergence, and the visual scene is changed from the sterile engraving of Veggie Corp's control to a dynamic embroidery of obstruction and versatility. Metropolitan spaces, once meaningful of similarity, presently bear the characteristics of insubordination. Landmarks rise, embellished with images that recognize the battle for opportunity. The story explores the fastidious fix of foundation, the reclamation of fundamental administrations, and the rise of another visual character for the freed society. It turns into a reflection on the versatile limit of the human soul, as the once-mistreated masses effectively partake in forming the actual sign of their newly discovered independence.

The freed society, having risen up out of the cauldron of contention, wrestles with the intricacies of administration and the detailing of another world request. The characters, push into influential positions by the exigencies of insubordination, become modelers of a general public that tries to limit any association with the shadows of Veggie Corp's severe rule. The story investigates the foundation of new administration structures, the fragile harmony between individual independence and aggregate request, and the difficulties of keeping a freed society. The method involved with revamping turns into a story space for looking at the subtleties of initiative, administration, and the desires of a general public that has tasted opportunity after delayed oppression.

The story ceases from introducing an idealistic vision of the post-struggle world, deliberately presenting the intricacies and difficulties innate in remaking society. Power vacuums, factional debates, and the leftovers of Veggie Corp's impact make an embroidery of unseen conflicts that highlight the delicacy of freedom. The characters, when joined in their rebellion against a shared adversary, presently face the complexities of post-struggle administration, exploring the unfamiliar domains of cultural reproduction. The account catches the strain among vision and sober mindedness, stressing that the freed society isn't safe to the entanglements that go with the mission for independence.

Underlying changes inside the freed society reach out past the actual domain, saturating the philosophical and social texture. The story investigates the development of new philosophies, developments, and voices that shape the forms of the post-Veggie Corp period. The freed masses, when hushed by the vegetable masters, presently add to a different and dynamic talk. The story winds around strings of philosophical variety, mirroring the horde points of view that arise in the repercussions of contention. The remaking turns into a story space for investigating the conflict and juncture of thoughts, passing on space for the cultural development to unfurl in unforeseen bearings.

As the characters explore the intricacies of remaking, their own changes keep on unfurling. The scars, wins, and advancing comprehension of their jobs in the reshaped tragic world become necessary to the recreation story. Connections inside the obstruction group develop further, mirroring the persevering through bonds fashioned in the pot of contention. The brotherhood, tried by the power of the disobedience, changes into more profound associations in light of shared encounters and the aggregate weight of their victorious stand. The account investigates the close to home scene of the characters, digging into their weaknesses, yearnings, and the developing elements that characterize the post-struggle time.

The charming head of Veggie Corp, however crushed, keeps on creating a waiting shaded area in the repercussions. The remainders of Veggie Corp endeavor to refocus, presenting a component of vulnerability and pressure.

The crushed pioneer's heritage turns into a story impetus, as the freed society wrestles with the disclosures about Veggie Corp's dull insider facts and the genuine inspirations driving the vegetable masters. The story interlaces the self-improvement account with the more extensive cultural changes, featuring the interconnectedness of individual excursions and the general battle against harsh control.

Unforeseen difficulties arise as a story impetus, testing the strength of the recently freed society and becoming pots for additional person improvement. The remainders of Veggie Corp, however crushed in the actual sense, keep on applying impact through clandestine tasks and endeavors to take advantage of weaknesses. The story explores the unseen conflicts inside the freed society — factional debates, power vacuums, and the intricacies of exploring a world untethered from the general control of vegetable masters. The recreation story turns into a reflection on the repeating idea of contention and the persevering through difficulties that go with the mission for enduring opportunity.

In the account's investigation of reconstructing society, the visual portrayal of the tragic world advances. The once-motorized, sterile designs currently become materials for creative articulation, mirroring the freed society's dismissal of consistency and similarity. The account catches the change of Veggie Corp's foundation into energetic centers of imagination, local area, and uniqueness. The freed society, having broken the shackles of uniform control, recovers its independence in administration as well as in the actual quintessence of its social and visual character.

As the story works toward its intelligent end result, the characters and society stand at the junction of another section. The fallout turns into a space for reflection, festivity, and affirmation of the results, forfeits, and persevering through effect of the disobedience. The story ceases from introducing a flawlessly tied-up goal, leaving specific strings purposely unconditional. The freed society, however liberated from Veggie Corp's quick control, turns into a story vessel for future experiences, improvements, and neglected regions.

9.1 Explore how the defeat of Veggie Corp leads to a restructuring of society.

The loss of Veggie Corp in "Green Conflicts: The Veggie Feud" proclaims a seismic change in the tragic world, making way for the rebuilding of society. As the vegetable masters are vanquished, the story changes into a convincing investigation of the freed society's excursion towards independence, administration, and the reshaping of cultural designs. The loss turns into an impetus, for the destruction of harsh control as well as for the rise of another request, as the freed masses wrestle with the intricacies of recreation.

The visual scene goes through an extreme change, representing the freed society's dismissal of Veggie Corp's sterile control. Metropolitan spaces, when overwhelmed by the harsh impact of vegetable masters, demonstrate the veracity of the introduction of opposition and imagination. Landmarks to opposition rise, decorated with images of opportunity, denoting the finish of consistency and the start of a different and dynamic social articulation. The story dives into the fastidious course of recovering public spaces, reusing Veggie Corp's framework, and outwardly articulating the newly discovered independence. This visual transformation becomes significant of the general public's assurance to break liberated from the shackles of similarity and affirm its independence.

The recreation of society stretches out past the actual domain, digging into the philosophical texture that characterizes the freed world. The loss of Veggie Corp opens up spaces for the rise of new belief systems, developments, and voices. The story investigates the conflict and conjunction of thoughts, catching the philosophical variety that blooms directly following struggle. The freed masses, when hushed by the vegetable masters, presently take part in a unique talk that shapes the forms of their reshaped society. The rebuilding turns into a story space for looking at the nuanced embroidery of convictions and dreams that characterize the freed world.

The loss of Veggie Corp requires a reconsideration of administration structures, and the story drenches itself in the intricacies of post-struggle administration. The characters, push into influential positions by the defiance, become engineers of a general public that looks to move away from the shadows of Veggie Corp's harsh system. The story explores the sensitive harmony between individual independence and aggregate request, displaying the characters' battles to lay out an administration model that mirrors the goals of the freed society. The rebuilding turns into a story investigation of the complexities of authority, the developing idea of power, and the difficulties innate in keeping a freed society.

The freed society wrestles with the tradition of Veggie Corp, and the loss turns into an impetus for uncovering the dull insider facts and secret plans that characterized the vegetable masters' standard. The story investigates the most common way of destroying Veggie Corp's framework, uncovering the systems of control, and considering those liable for mistreatment responsible. The disclosures become a story figuring, underscoring the significance of straightforwardness and responsibility in the reshaped society. The loss of Veggie Corp frees the general public from actual control as well as turns into an emblematic victory over the hidden plots that once kept the majority in the hold of dread.

Startling difficulties arise in the result of Veggie Corp's loss, trying the versatility of the freed society and adding layers of intricacy to the rebuilding account. Power vacuums, factional questions, and remainders of Veggie Corp's impact make pressure inside the freed world.

The characters, having conquered the outer danger of the vegetable masters, presently explore the subtle conflicts that go with the mission for independence. The rebuilding story turns into a reflection on the delicacy of freedom, underscoring that the way to independence is full of difficulties that request watchfulness, versatility, and solidarity.

The individual changes saw in the characters keep on unfurling in the consequence of Veggie Corp's loss. The scars and wins of the resistance become fundamental to the rebuilding account, as the characters wrestle with their developing jobs in the reshaped society. Connections inside the opposition group advance further, mirroring the persevering through bonds fashioned in the cauldron of contention. The kinship, tried by the power of the defiance, changes into more profound associations in view of shared encounters and the aggregate weight of their victorious stand. The account digs into the close to home scene of the characters, investigating their weaknesses, goals, and the developing elements that characterize the post-struggle time.

The magnetic head of Veggie Corp, however crushed, keeps on creating a waiting shaded area in the result. The remainders of Veggie Corp endeavor to refocus, presenting a component of vulnerability and strain. The story investigates the crushed pioneer's heritage, winding around an account string that clues at the potential for waiting shadows and neglected profundities. The rebuilding becomes a physical and philosophical cycle as well as a story investigation of the mental effect of Veggie Corp's impact on the freed society.

As the story works toward its intelligent end result, the rebuilding of society turns into a material for contemplation, festivity, and affirmation of the outcomes, forfeits, and persevering through effect of the defiance. The characters and society stand at the intersection of another part, and the rebuilding story turns into a space for examining the fragile balance among past and future. The story ceases from introducing a conveniently tied-up goal, leaving specific strings intentionally unassuming. The freed society, having broken the shackles of Veggie Corp's quick control, turns into a story vessel for future experiences, improvements, and neglected regions.

1. **Highlight the challenges and opportunities that arise as people transition away from vegetable dominance.**

The change away from vegetable predominance in "Green Conflicts: The Veggie Feud" denotes a vital stage in the reshaping of the tragic world. As the story unfurls, it digs into the difficulties and valuable open doors that emerge in the result of Veggie Corp's loss, investigating the intricacies of weaning society off its reliance on vegetables and embracing a freshly discovered independence.

One of the focal difficulties that arises in this momentary period is the calculated shift away from vegetable-based foundation. For quite a long time, Veggie Corp had laid out a firmly controlled framework where vegetables served as a wellspring of force as well as for the purpose of food and control. The account explores the hardships of destroying this profoundly settled in framework, tending to the pragmatic difficulties of supplanting vegetable-based energy sources, reconsidering agrarian practices, and reconfiguring cultural designs worked around vegetable predominance. The freedom from vegetable control requests an extensive update of the current frameworks, giving the general public the impressive errand of adjusting to elective wellsprings of force and food.

The philosophical shift away from vegetable predominance additionally acts difficulties like the freed society wrestles with the mental outcome of Veggie Corp's impact. The account investigates how the imbued faith in the predominance of vegetables as rulers and suppliers influences the shared awareness. Conquering the mental molding turns into an obstacle as the general public changes toward an additional decent and different point of view. The story dives into the obstruction looked by the individuals who find it trying to break liberated from the well established belief systems that situated vegetables as considerate masters. The test lies in destroying actual designs as well as in freeing minds from the well established impact of vegetable strength.

The monetary repercussions of the progress away from vegetable strength become a huge point of convergence in the story. Veggie Corp had firmly controlled the economy, with vegetables filling in as both cash and item. The loss of Veggie Corp presents a time of financial vulnerability as the freed society wrestles with the need to lay out new exchange practices, monetary standards, and financial designs. The story explores the intricacies of progressing from a vegetable-driven economy to one that values variety, development, and the commitments of different enterprises. The monetary rebuilding becomes both a chance for newly discovered success and a test as the general public adjusts to a more adjusted and fair framework.

In the midst of the difficulties, valuable open doors for development and variety emerge as the freed society rethinks its relationship with assets and advances. The story investigates the potential for elective energy sources, feasible farming practices, and innovative progressions that were stifled influenced quite a bit by control. The progress turns into a material for inventiveness and advancement as people, when compelled by vegetable strength, presently have the opportunity to investigate and foster a wide cluster of innovations and practices. The story winds around a story of flexibility, versatility, and the human limit with regards to inventiveness when unburdened by the limits forced by a severe system.

The cultural rebuilding additionally delivers the chance for social rejuvenation. Veggie Corp had forced a solid culture that smothered variety and individual articulation. The loss of Veggie Corp takes into consideration the resurgence of different social practices, imaginative articulations, and a rich embroidery of customs that were stifled during the period of vegetable predominance.

The story praises the freshly discovered opportunity to embrace and celebrate different social personalities, cultivating a feeling of solidarity in variety. The momentary period turns into a period of social investigation, rediscovery, and the affirmation of the magnificence that emerges when individuals are allowed to communicate their novel characters.

Social elements go through a groundbreaking movement as the freed society reconsiders relational connections and local area structures. The account investigates the open doors for more noteworthy inclusivity, co-ordinated effort, and the breakdown of inflexible orders that were kept up with by Veggie Corp. The loss of the vegetable masters turns into an impetus for producing new associations, coalitions, and an aggregate feeling of direction. The difficulties of the progress become open doors for building a more populist and interconnected society where people are enabled to contribute their abilities, information, and encounters without the requirements forced by vegetable predominance.

Natural contemplations become the overwhelming focus as the account tends to the biological effect of progressing away from vegetable strength. The period of Veggie Corp had seen the abuse and control of regular assets to support vegetables. The freed society currently faces the open door and challenge of laying out reasonable practices that focus on ecological preservation. The story investigates the fragile harmony between bridling the World's assets for human necessities while protecting the sensitive biological balance. The change turns into a chance for the general public to rethink its relationship with nature, gaining from the missteps of the past and taking a stab at congruity with the climate.

The story finishes up with a nuanced investigation of the sensitive harmony between the difficulties and potential open doors that characterize the momentary period away from vegetable predominance. The freed society remains at the limit of another period, having defeated the severe control of Veggie Corp. The difficulties presented by destroying instilled frameworks and philosophies are met with flexibility, imagination, and the assurance to fashion a general public that embraces variety and opportunity. The potential open doors for development, social rejuvenation, financial thriving, and natural stewardship become encouraging signs, directing the freed society toward a future unshackled from the shadows of vegetable predominance. Eventually, the story welcomes perusers to ponder the perplexing dance among difficulties and open doors as the tragic world goes through a significant and extraordinary renaissance.

9.2 The Legacy of the Veggie Vendetta

The tradition of the Veggie Feud in "Green Conflicts: The Veggie Quarrel" turns into a strong investigation of the persevering through influence, illustrations learned, and the permanent imprint left on the tragic world.

As the account unfurls, it dives into the broad results of the insubordination to Veggie Corp, analyzing how the victory over vegetable predominance resonates through the freed society, forming its direction, and impacting the shared mindset.

One of the focal parts of the Veggie Grudge's heritage lies in the freshly discovered independence and flexibility of the freed society. The loss of Veggie Corp addresses an emblematic breaking of chains, liberating the majority from the severe control of vegetable masters. The account catches the quintessence of strengthening as people, once enslaved and hushed, presently get comfortable with themselves and organization in molding the heading of their general public. The heritage turns into a demonstration of the steady human soul, showing that even notwithstanding imposing chances, obstruction and aggregate activity can prompt victory.

The story unfurls as a reflection on the examples gained from the Veggie Quarrel, stressing the significance of carefulness, solidarity, and the tireless quest for opportunity. The difficulties looked during the insubordination act as a pot for individual and aggregate development, imparting a feeling of flexibility that turns into a foundation of the freed society. The heritage turns into a vault of shrewdness, an update that the seeds of progress can develop in the most severe soils, and that the battle for independence requests persistent exertion and cautiousness.

The loss of Veggie Corp likewise makes a permanent imprint on the cultural designs that arise in the result. The freed society wrestles with the chance to lay out an administration model that values straightforwardness, inclusivity, and the interest of its residents. The account explores the intricacies of this change, investigating how the examples gained from the Veggie Feud educate the recreation regarding administration structures. The heritage turns into a story space for looking at the sensitive harmony between individual opportunities and aggregate liabilities, shaping a general public that protective elements against the resurgence of severe control.

Socially, the tradition of the Veggie Feud ignites a renaissance, commending variety, and restoring customs smothered during Veggie Corp's standard. The story catches the liveliness of a general public that rediscovers its character, embracing the lavishness of different social articulations. Imaginative undertakings, writing, and social practices that were once smothered by vegetable strength presently thrive, turning into a fundamental piece of the freed society's legacy. The heritage turns into a festival of the human soul's ability to persevere and flourish, even notwithstanding harsh control.

Monetarily, the Veggie Feud's inheritance prompts a recalibration of exchange rehearses and financial designs. The freed society, unshackled from the limitations of a vegetable-driven economy, investigates open doors for development, maintainability, and fair dispersion of assets.

The account looks at how the examples from the defiance illuminate monetary approaches that focus on the prosperity of the general population and the dependable utilization of assets. The inheritance turns into a story focal point through which financial practices are reconsidered, encouraging flourishing and guaranteeing that the errors of the past are not rehashed.

Natural contemplations assume a critical part in the tradition of the Veggie Feud. The loss of Veggie Corp prompts a restored obligation to natural stewardship, as the freed society wrestles with the outcomes of past biological double-dealing. The account investigates the general public's undertaking to lay out feasible practices that orchestrate with the climate. The inheritance turns into a source of inspiration, motivating an aggregate liability to safeguard the planet for people in the future. It turns into a story string that meshes natural cognizance into the texture of the freed society's personality.

The loss of Veggie Corp's chief and the openness of the vegetable masters' dull privileged insights add to the heritage by encouraging an aggregate consciousness of the risks of unrestrained power and the significance of responsibility. The story investigates how the examples from the Veggie Grudge shape the freed society's way to deal with initiative, imparting a pledge to straightforwardness and forestalling the centralization of force in the possession of a couple. The inheritance turns into a protect against the reappearance of dictator control, filling in as an update that opportunity requests everlasting cautiousness.

The relational elements and connections fashioned during the Veggie Grudge leave an enduring effect on the freed society. The story investigates how the securities framed in the cauldron of contention become an establishment for a more interconnected and compassionate local area. The heritage turns into a story space for looking at the getting through strength of connections, underscoring that the victory over Veggie Corp was an aggregate undertaking as well as a demonstration of the profound human associations manufactured even with misfortune.

1. **Examine how the events of the Veggie Vendetta have left a lasting impact on the world.**

    The occasions of the Veggie Feud in "Green Conflicts: The Veggie Quarrel" resound a long ways past the bounds of the story, leaving a permanent and enduring effect on the tragic world it possesses. The story unfurls as a significant assessment of how the victory over Veggie Corp resounds through the freed society, reshaping its direction, philosophies, and the shared perspective.

The most substantial and quick effect of the Veggie Grudge lies in the recently discovered feeling of independence and opportunity that penetrates the freed society. The harsh rule of Veggie Corp is vanquished, and the account catches the instinctive snapshot of liberation as the majority cast off the shackles of vegetable strength. This seismic change in power elements turns into an extremely important occasion, imparting an aggregate soul of strength and strengthening. The enduring effect is clear in the freed society's self-assuredness, as people, once oppressed, arise as modelers of their own fates, forming the world over again with a feeling of organization and reason.

The Veggie Feud turns into a pot of examples learned, and its effect resonates through the reproduction of administration structures. The story explores the intricacies of laying out another request, one that values straightforwardness, inclusivity, and responsibility. The tradition of the defiance turns into a directing power in the freed society's way to deal with authority, encouraging a pledge to forestalling the convergence of force and guaranteeing that the mix-ups of the past are not rehashed. The effect is felt in the general public's strength against tyrant propensities, making a defend against the resurgence of harsh control.

Socially, the Veggie Grudge starts a renaissance, reviving different social articulations that had been stifled under Veggie Corp's standard. The story unfurls as a festival of the huge number of voices and customs that were smothered during the period of vegetable predominance. The freed society embraces social variety, cultivating a climate where imaginative undertakings, writing, and conventional practices prosper. The effect is clear in the lively embroidery of a revitalized social character, woven with strings of flexibility, variety, and the extravagance of aggregate legacy.

Financially, the Veggie Grudge prompts a recalibration of exchange rehearses and monetary designs. The freed society, unshackled from the requirements of a vegetable-driven economy, investigates open doors for development, manageability, and fair circulation of assets. The story inspects how the examples from the insubordination illuminate financial approaches that focus on the prosperity of the general population and the capable utilization of assets. The effect is found in the general public's flexibility, versatility, and obligation to building a monetary system that values flourishing without compromising the standards of opportunity and value.

Natural contemplations assume a huge part in the getting through effect of the Veggie Grudge. The loss of Veggie Corp prompts a recharged obligation to natural stewardship as the freed society wrestles with the results of past biological double-dealing. The account unfurls as an investigation of the general public's undertaking to lay out feasible practices that fit with the climate. The effect is obvious in the aggregate liability to safeguard the planet for people in the future, making a story string that meshes natural cognizance into the texture of the freed society's personality.

The loss of Veggie Corp's chief and the openness of the vegetable masters' dull privileged insights add to an enduring effect by encouraging an aggregate familiarity with the risks of unrestrained power and the significance of responsibility. The story investigates how the examples from the Veggie Grudge shape the freed society's way to deal with authority, imparting a guarantee to straightforwardness and forestalling the convergence of force in the possession of a couple. The effect turns into a defend against the reappearance of tyrant control, filling in as an update that opportunity requests everlasting watchfulness.

Relational elements and connections fashioned during the Veggie Grudge leave a persevering through influence on the freed society. The story investigates how the securities shaped in the cauldron of contention become an establishment for a more interconnected and sympathetic local area. The effect is felt in the general public's aggregate strength, underscoring that the victory over

Veggie Corp was an aggregate undertaking as well as a demonstration of the profound human associations manufactured notwithstanding misfortune. The persevering through influence is clear in the manner people connect with each other, encouraging a feeling of local area, common help, and a common obligation to protecting the hard-won opportunities.

2. **Discuss the lessons learned and the lingering effects on the characters and society.**

The examples gained from the Veggie Grudge in "Green Conflicts: The Veggie Feud" are significant, forming the characters and society in manners that stretch out a long ways past the quick victory over Veggie Corp. As the story unfurls, it turns into an intelligent investigation of the persevering through effect of these examples and the waiting consequences for the characters and the general public they occupy.

One of the central examples that reverberates all through the story is the unstoppable force of aggregate activity. The characters, once mistreated by the mind-boggling could of Veggie Corp, discover that solidarity, versatility, and a common obligation to opportunity can win over apparently outlandish chances. The waiting impacts of this example are obvious in the changed society, where a feeling of aggregate reason and fortitude becomes imbued. People who once worked in separation track down strength in their interconnectedness, encouraging a general public that values joint effort and common help as fundamental mainstays of flexibility.

The Veggie Grudge grants an example on the significance of cautiousness and the unending battle for opportunity. Characters and society the same discover that the battle against mistreatment is certainly not a one-time occasion yet a continuous cycle that requests persistent exertion and mindfulness.

The story unfurls as a wake up call, reminding the freed society that the leftovers of Veggie Corp's impact might wait, requiring timeless carefulness to forestall the reappearance of tyrant control. This illustration turns into a core value, forming the cultural mentality and empowering an aggregate obligation to defending the hard-won opportunities.

Straightforwardness and responsibility arise as urgent examples gained from the Veggie Grudge. The characters wrestle with the results of Veggie Corp's mysterious rule and the control of data. The story investigates how this acknowledgment fills a pledge to straightforwardness in administration and an interest for responsibility. The waiting impacts are apparent in the recreated cultural designs, where pioneers are held to better expectations, and the smoke screen that once covered people with significant influence is lifted. The illustration turns into a foundation of the freed society's ethos, guaranteeing that straightforwardness stays a non-debatable part of administration.

The characters go through a significant change as they incorporate the example that singular organization is a strong power against oppression. The story unfurls as an excursion of self-disclosure, where characters who once felt weak come to understand the power of their decisions and activities. The waiting impacts are found in the enabled people who, having tasted the pleasantness of opportunity, become dynamic supporters of the reshaped society. This illustration turns into an impetus for self-awareness and cultural change, underscoring that each individual has the ability to impact the course of history.

Social rejuvenation turns into an example gained from the Veggie Quarrel, as characters and society rediscover the worth of different social articulations. The story unfurls as a festival of individual and aggregate social personalities, investigating how the concealment of social variety under Veggie Corp's standard smothered imagination and development. The waiting impacts are apparent in the energetic social scene that arises in the freed society, where imaginative undertakings, writing, and customary practices thrive. The example turns into a demonstration of the flexibility of social legacy and the extraordinary force of embracing variety.

Financial recalibration turns into a functional example as characters and society explore the reproduction of monetary designs. The story investigates the difficulties and open doors innate in moving away from a vegetable-driven economy. The waiting impacts are found in the freed society's obligation to building a financial structure that focuses on fair appropriation of assets, maintainability, and the prosperity of its general population. This illustration turns into a plan for financial practices that line up with the standards of opportunity and decency.

Natural stewardship arises as an illustration with enduring consequences for characters and society. The story depicts the outcomes of Veggie Corp's biological double-dealing and the ensuing obligation to mindful ecological practices.

The waiting impacts are apparent in the general public's commitment to safeguarding the planet for people in the future. This example turns into a core value, encouraging an aggregate liability to orchestrate human exercises with the sensitive biological equilibrium.

Relational connections are profoundly influenced by the examples gained from the Veggie Grudge. Characters, having fashioned bonds in the pot of contention, convey the getting through impacts of these connections into the reshaped society. The story investigates how the brotherhood and shared help created during the insubordination become primary components of the freed society's social texture. The example turns into a demonstration of the strength of human associations and the extraordinary force of fortitude.

9.3 A Glimpse into the Future

A brief look into the fate of the tragic world following the occasions of "Green Conflicts: The Veggie Feud" uncovers a changed scene, reverberating with the reverberations of disobedience and versatility. The story unfurls as a speculative investigation of the getting through effect of the Veggie Quarrel, offering a window into the cultural, social, financial, and ecological movements that shape the direction of the freed world.

In the cultural domain, the freed world arises as a stronghold of opportunity and participatory administration. The illustrations gained from the Veggie Grudge become imbued in the cultural ethos, molding an administration model that values straightforwardness, inclusivity, and responsibility. The story offers a brief look into decentralized dynamic cycles, where the voices of people are heard, and pioneers are held to the honest best expectations. The freed society turns into a signal of majority rule standards, delineating how the victory over Veggie Corp established the groundwork for a general public where power is circulated among individuals.

Socially, the freed world encounters a lively renaissance, commending the variety of voices and articulations smothered during Veggie Corp's standard. The story unfurls as an embroidery woven with the strings of imaginative undertakings, writing, and conventional practices that once mulled in lack of clarity. A brief look into what's in store uncovers social celebrations, displays, and a prospering of imagination that becomes symbolic of the freed society's obligation to embracing and commending its rich social legacy. The reverberations of the Veggie Quarrel resound in each stroke of paint, each note of music, and each word wrote in recently discovered abstract opportunity.

Monetarily, the freed society outlines a course toward supportability and impartial flourishing. A brief look into what's in store uncovers monetary practices that focus on the prosperity of the general population and dependable asset the executives. The story investigates the development of creative businesses, advancements, and exchange rehearses that twist the shortfall of Veggie Corp's prohibitive monetary designs.

The freed society turns into a demonstration of the strength of its kin, producing a financial structure that values variety, moral practices, and the aggregate thriving of its residents.

Natural stewardship becomes the dominant focal point as a foundation of the freed society's personality. A brief look into what's in store uncovers an existence where the examples gained from Veggie Corp's biological double-dealing have converted into a profound obligation to ecological protection. The story unfurls as an investigation of reasonable practices, sustainable power sources, and an amicable conjunction with the normal world. The freed society turns into a gatekeeper of the planet, endeavoring to mend the scars left by Veggie Corp and guaranteeing that people in the future acquire an existence where natural equilibrium is saved.

Relational connections keep on flourishing in the freed society, mirroring the getting through strength of the bonds fashioned during the Veggie Quarrel. A brief look into what's in store uncovers networks based on trust, compassion, and a common obligation to aggregate prosperity. The story investigates how the illustrations gained from the disobedience become a basic piece of the freed society's social texture, cultivating a feeling of solidarity that rises above individual contrasts. The freed world turns into a demonstration of the groundbreaking force of human associations, where the scars of contention are supplanted by the recuperating salve of shared help and fellowship.

While the freed world flourishes, a brief look into what's in store likewise recognizes the difficulties that endure. The story investigates the remainders of Veggie Corp's impact, unpretentious shadows that wait in the cultural mind and epic showdowns that compromise the sensitive balance. The freed society faces the continuous errand of protecting its hard-won opportunities, exploring inside questions, and staying cautious against any expected resurgence of dictator control. The future, however splendid, isn't without its intricacies, and the story unfurls as a demonstration of the freed society's strength despite developing difficulties.

1. **Provide a sneak peek into what lies ahead for the characters and the world they've reshaped.**

   As the drapery falls on the wild occasions of "Green Conflicts: The Veggie Quarrel," a slip look into what's to come offers a tempting look at what lies ahead for the characters and the world they've all in all reshaped. The story unfurls as a speculative excursion, winding around together strings of self-awareness, cultural change, and the consistently present reverberations of the Veggie Feud.

In the repercussions of the disobedience, the characters set out on individual odysseys of self-disclosure and recuperating. The sneak look uncovers their own directions, uncovering how the scars of the Veggie Grudge become impetuses for development. The once hesitant legend, driven by an individual feud, tracks down comfort in the newly discovered opportunity to investigate life past the shackles of persecution. Each character wrestles with the waiting impacts of their past, exploring complex feelings, and outlining courses toward reclamation and reason.

Culturally, the freed world turns into a material for the characters' aggregate endeavors to fabricate a perfect world out of the remains of Veggie Corp's oppression. The sneak look unfurls as an excursion through clamoring commercial centers where different voices reverberation in exuberant discussions. The story investigates the recreated administration structures, showing how the examples gained from the Veggie Grudge illuminate a framework where power is shared, choices are straightforward, and pioneers are considered responsible. Residents effectively partake in molding the future, highlighting the freed society's obligation to the standards of a majority rules system and aggregate organization.

Socially, the sneak look uncovers a kaleidoscope of imaginative articulations that twist in the freed world. Roads embellished with energetic wall paintings, theaters exhibiting assorted exhibitions, and libraries overflowing with writing become images of social restoration. The characters, once quieted, presently add to this social renaissance, reviving stories and customs that Veggie Corp looked to eradicate. The freed society turns into a demonstration of the versatility of social character, where each brushstroke and each tune is a festival of newly discovered opportunity.

Monetarily, the sneak look represents a scene of development and maintainable thriving. The characters, having destroyed Veggie Corp's monetary extremely tight grip, encourage a climate where business flourishes. The account investigates expanding ventures zeroed in on moral practices, sustainable assets, and evenhanded appropriation of riches. The freed society turns into a model for financial strength, exhibiting how the examples of the past have prepared for a future where flourishing is shared and based on standards of reasonableness.

Natural stewardship stays a point of convergence in the sneak look, displaying a world that has gained from Veggie Corp's biological offenses. The story unfurls in lavish scenes where green advances saddle the force of nature without abuse. Sustainable power sources, dependable agrarian practices, and preservation endeavors become vital pieces of the freed society's obligation to saving the climate. The sneak look offers a dream of an existence where the scars of ecological corruption are recuperating, and the planet flourishes close by a general public that values its fragile equilibrium.

Relational connections keep on developing in the sneak look, representing the persevering through strength of associations produced during the Veggie Grudge. Networks bond over shared encounters, making organizations of help and fortitude. The story investigates the characters' continuous excursions to accommodate with their pasts and structure further associations with each other. The freed world turns into a demonstration of the extraordinary force of human connections, where sympathy, understanding, and aggregate reason weave the structure holding the system together.

Notwithstanding, the sneak look likewise recognizes the difficulties that endure in the freed world. The characters, while victorious, face the intricacies of revamping a general public scarred by Veggie Corp's standard. Waiting biases, epic showdowns, and outer dangers present imposing obstructions. The story unfurls with a feeling of strain, proposing that the reverberations of the Veggie Grudge keep on resonating, requesting the characters' proceeded with cautiousness and versatility.

2. **Tease potential new challenges or adventures, keeping the door open for future stories in the Green Wars universe.**

As the characters luxuriate in the phosphorescence of their victory over Veggie Corp, an unobtrusive pressure waits all around, indicating likely new difficulties and undertakings that might shape the Green Conflicts universe in the days to come. The story unfurls with a feeling of expectation, passing on the entryway slightly open for future stories to investigate the strange regions of this tragic world.

The freed society, while delighting in newly discovered opportunity, wrestles with the intricacies of revamping. The slip look into what's in store proposes that the scars left by Veggie Corp's standard run profound, making separation points inside the cultural texture. Waiting biases and feelings of disdain stew underneath the surface, compromising the hard-won solidarity accomplished during the Veggie Grudge. The account prods the potential for unseen fits of turmoil that might test the flexibility of the freed world, unwinding stowed away difficulties that request aggregate contemplation and goal.

Monetary recalibration, however a victory, opens a Pandora's container of unexpected difficulties. The sneak look alludes to outside powers that try to take advantage of the weaknesses of the freed society. New players enter the stage, their thought processes covered in secret, and financial coalitions become delicate as the characters explore a scene where old enemies might be supplanted by new dangers. The story proposes that the freed society's excursion toward monetary independence might be full of unexpected deterrents, making way for another part in the Green Conflicts universe.

Ecological stewardship, a foundation of the freed society's personality, faces outside pressures that strain its obligation to manageability. The sneak look discloses an existence where the fragile harmony between human advancement and natural protection is dubious. The story alludes to shadowy substances that look to take advantage of the climate for their benefit, testing the characters' purpose to safeguard the planet. As the freed society wrestles with outside dangers to its natural ethos, the stage is set for an environmental fight that might shape the eventual fate of the Green Conflicts universe.

The social renaissance, while flourishing, isn't resistant to outer impacts that challenge the freed society's obligation to variety. The sneak look alludes to philosophical conflicts, as leftovers of Veggie Corp's philosophy endeavor to penetrate the social scene. Characters wind up at the very front of a social conflict, where the stories they battled to restore face outside endeavors at concealment. The story recommends that the freed society should stay watchful, safeguarding social personality against outer powers try to delete the hard-won triumphs of the Veggie Grudge.

Relational connections, however fortified, face new tests in the advancing scene of the freed world. The sneak look investigates the intricacies of unique interactions stressed by outside pressures. Characters explore difficulties that test the bonds manufactured during the Veggie Feud, as new unions are framed and old loyalties are addressed. The account alludes to the delicacy of relational elements even with outer impacts, prodding likely contentions and partnerships that might rethink the characters' excursions in the Green Conflicts universe.

The initiative of the freed society, once joined against a shared adversary, faces the innate difficulties of administration. The sneak look digs into the intricacies of direction, where unique sentiments compete for noticeable quality. Characters, when joined in the battle against Veggie Corp, wind up in conflict over the bearing of the freed society. The story proposes that the way to another world request is overflowing with inside discusses, fights for control, and philosophical conflicts that might shape the future direction of the Green Conflicts universe.